CAMP BESTIVAL

AT HOME

EBURY
PRESS

JOSIE & ROB DA BANK

CAMP BESTIVAL

AT HOME

HAVE A FAMILY
FESTIVAL EVERY DAY

CONTENTS

To say that Camp Bestival is our proudest achievement is probably a huge understatement. To somehow have stumbled across a way of life (I'm not sure we have ever thought of it as a proper job) that has meant Josie and I can work together on an insanely creative ever-evolving art and music project that pops up in a field once (and now twice) a year ... and one that has included all our kids' upbringings, musical education and hopefully future work ethic is nothing short of a gift.

Yes it's been incredibly stressful at times and 'living the festival life' can get a bit trying in close family quarters, much like watching a novice family of five sharing an accidentally purchased three-person tent at a festival for the first time ... but we wouldn't change the last 15 years of polite partying, arguments in the office, late-night dad raving, dancing like no one's watching, changing stinky nappies on the back of a moving golf buggy in a muddy field, kids having tantrums over who owns a stick, dressing up as a vegetable or imaginary space object to try and win the fancy dress competition or even checking portaloos at 2am to see if there's any room left for people to sit down.

This book is intended to hopefully capture some of the magic of the festival, the art, the colour, the vibrant, noisy in-ya-face ups and downs of festival life which we can all practice at home ... wherever we live, in whatever kind of dwelling and on any budget. Please don't imagine that the da Bank clan live some utopian life sitting round an ecologically sound campfire toasting marshmallows and singing folk songs to each other. Our kids are allowed to fall back on tablets and TVs and yes we occasionally eat frozen meals and naughty things made from chocolate too, but this book will hopefully give us all some inspiration of how we can live a fun, alternative lifestyle now and again and one that our kids will thank us for.

This book is designed as a kind of annual or almanac (posh word for a book that reflects different things happening throughout the year) and is meant to be picked up and put down many times a year for practical help (recipes and things to make and do) as well as diversionary tactics so please don't feel you need to nail it all in one go. Like a well curated festival, it's something that you can explore at your leisure and each time you might discover a little hidden corner of wisdom or a spark of inspiration. It was a lot of fun writing this book and we hope you make some magical memories and have incredible adventures after reading it.

Robby and Josie

INTRODUCTION
to dressing up as a family

Robby and I set up Bestival in 2004, and one of the first things we decided was that Saturday would be Fancy Dress Day, with a big themed parade. We have stuck with this ever since. In fact, we were so blown away by the creativity and effort that in 2011, we published a book called *The Art of Dressing Up*. Even the artists used to dress up. Florence and the Machine, Lily Allen, Mika and the Scissor Sisters absolutely nailed it – among many others. Each year, we give Camp Bestival a theme to help inspire families, such as 'Animal Snap' or 'Aliens and Space'.

I think dressing up allows you to become someone different for the day – especially us grumpy old parents! It encourages us to let go of our uptight qualities and have FUN. I think the best outfits are homemade and upcycled, and what I really love the most is when a family arrives with a group costume. Last year, a family came to Shropshire dressed as Excel spreadsheets – genius and simple to make.

Here are our tips for dressing up as a family.

PLAN AHEAD

Hold a relaxed family meeting with no pressure. Just list out all your ideas and let the children's creativity run wild. Think about what you've already got at home, what you enjoy making, who's good at what. At this point, the parents can talk about who they have always wanted to be, and maybe do some impressions. You can either all go as individual characters, or as a group. Maybe you'll be lobsters, astronauts, vegetables, or the cast of a film ... I'm hoping to see some Thunderbirds this year.

GET CREATING

Once you've all decided who's going as what, see what you have at home to make the outfits. If you don't have what's needed, try to borrow items or go to your local charity shops before you buy an outfit off the internet. There is nothing wrong with buying a costume, but it's always good to start with reuse and go from there.

KEEP IT FUN

Don't forget you don't have to go the whole hog with your character. You can just use face paint, wigs, glitter, tails and capes to make you feel special. And, of course, you can just dress in your fave dress or outfit and accessorise. I find these days, especially living on an island, there aren't many opportunities to dress up in my best – so any excuse!

HAVE A DRESS REHEARSAL

Once the outfits are ready, have a dress rehearsal ... and perhaps a themed dinner to go with them.

Josie

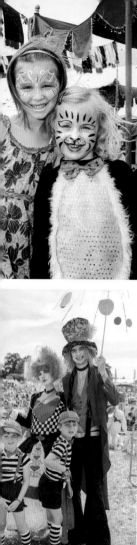

Introduction to .... STARGAZING

Did you know that the first people believed the stars to be golden nail-heads holding up the ceiling of the universe? Since then, stars have been used to predict the future, to divide our year into months and to steer ships across oceans. They have informed a large part of our culture and are central to advances in science. But you don't have to be a scientist or have expensive equipment to study the skies. Just look up!

To get started, choose a good place to gaze; somewhere away from light pollution and tall obstacles. If you can't get into the countryside, then football pitches, hills and parks are good as they offer an uncluttered horizon. Next, let your eyes get accustomed to the darkness — don't look at your phone, as this will ruin your night vision. As your eyes adapt, you will realise that some stars are brighter than others, and that some are different in colour too. This is because they are different distances away and burn at different temperatures. Most of them are white, but if you keep looking, you will see that some are more blue and others are more yellow or orange.

Our friend Steve at Gloucester Astronomy suggests that a good way to start is to identify a planet or constellation. This book starts in March by looking at Venus (page 20), because it is the brightest planet and very close to our moon, so it is easy to spot. Then, if you look down towards the horizon and slightly to the right, you should spot one of the oldest constellations in our sky; Ursa Major, or the Great Bear. From there, we try to look for another constellation that is near to the one you just found, so that you build up a map of stars as the year goes by. The constellations on view change during the year as the Earth rotates.

Some stars are quite faint, and so you may find it useful to take a good pair of binoculars with you. If you really develop an interest, why don't you join a local astronomy group? And don't forget that stargazing can be cold in the winter months, so wrap up warm!

FOREWORD

by Sara Cox

Camp Bestival at home, hey? It's the dream! Sure, we've taken our three children to Camp Bestival every year, from sweet toddlers all the way through to floppy-haired teens, so we're big fans — but the idea of distilling the magic of Camp Bestival, boiling it down to its very essence so it can be enjoyed within the confines of your own four walls (and, if you're lucky, a garden)? Well, that's just magic.

Camp Bestival is easily my family's favourite weekend of the year. We roam the site screen-free, full-bellied and blissed-out, and work stress and modern-day hamster-wheel freneticism seem a trillion light years away.

There's a problem, though — it's only available two weekends a year (and that's if you visit both Dorset and Shropshire).

Why should such carefree happiness, japes and jollies be squished into a few days of the year? WHY RATION JOY?

Now, with this book, the Camp Besti feeling can be enjoyed all year round, whenever the mood takes you. You have Access All Areas passes, so you can choose to dip your toe in or fully submerge yourself, depending on what tickles your fancy.

There are, of course, immediate upsides that spring to mind when using this book as opposed to visiting the festival in person.

You can flick through the pages while luxuriating in the knowledge that there is a loo close by — one you don't need to queue for. You are not at the mercy of the 'excitingly unseasonal' weather while reading this; come rain, shine or gale-force winds, you can snuggle somewhere with a brew, biscuits and this terrific tome.

You definitely won't need to use a sat nav while enjoying this book, which can only be a good thing; I heard a story that one year an idiot (me) accidentally drove three fractious children and a bewildered husband (my family) to Ludlow Castle in Shropshire (very much the wrong castle and county), where the only people around were two ladies in sensible shoes out for a walk). We found ourselves exactly 181 miles away from Lulworth Castle in Dorset (where Camp Bestival is held). I still maintain that eventually arriving at the festival at 2am was NOT 'traumatising' for our young children but was in fact 'character building'. (It's also worth noting that eight years after my moronic mess-up, Josie and Rob opened a second site — Camp Bestival SHROPSHIRE. Coincidence? I think not. In conclusion, I was just ahead of the curve.)

So, whether you visit the festival every year or you've never been, this book is your VIP ticket to enjoy everything that makes the festival the very best (the clue is in the name, babe). Josie and Rob have done a fantastic job of soaking every page with the sweet ingredients of Camp Bestival's vibe — the formula is a closely guarded family secret, but it's roughly a huge dollop of love blended with equal amounts of freedom to explore, some silly dancing, precious family time and magical memory-making, with a very liberal sprinkling of daftness and a dusting of nostalgia.

What better venue to enjoy all the good stuff that is waiting to be discovered within the pages of this special book than your own home? The place where you feel grounded, where the walls already sing with the laughter and chatter of your family, where you feel safe and loved.

So dive in, and enjoy every minute of your very own unique Camp Bestival at home.

Spr

We're lucky enough to live in the countryside, so we really see spring 'springing' at first-hand. We love colour and music, so from the green daffodil bulb optimistically peeking through the mud and dirt to noticing more birds testing out their songs in the brighter skies, it's always one of our favourite times of year. It's when we breathe a sigh of relief and look forward to longer days and a warmer sun. Bring on spring!

MARCH
did you know......

that that our lives run on Roman time? Their calendar months were named after Roman gods, leaders, festivals, and numbers. They named March after their god of war, Mars. They saw March as a month of new beginnings, so, like we have, they made it the first month of their calendar.

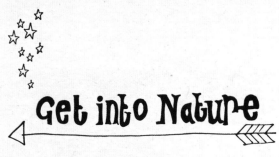

Get into Nature

Set your alarm, wrap up warm and try to identify the morning bird calls. Blackbirds are usually the first to sing, but with garden birds raising up to five broods between now and July, your garden may be filled with song for months! Try to identify the smaller garden birds such as robins, blue tits and sparrows, as they join in.

To help them find a safe place to nest, why not put up a birdbox?

WHAT ELSE?

Newborn lambs frolic in fields, while the 'white arse' wheatear is among the first returning birds that you can spot (almost) everywhere. And if you live in an area with hares, March is the best month to spot them before the grass grows. You may even be lucky enough to see them boxing.

You can also start to see the first spring flowers bloom. Have you noticed that most of them are yellow? If you're on a walk, look for primroses, celandines and daffodils as they emerge from hedges and on roadsides.

Foraging

Nettles can be found everywhere and are very nutritious, with high levels of vitamins A and C. You can make them into a soup, or use them like spinach. Check for nettles in the corners of your garden, in hedges, around trees and in untended grass areas. Cut the young leaves from the top of the plants using gloves and scissors.

Violets are delicious mixed into a rice pudding or used as a decoration. To forage for them, look in the undergrowth, as they like shady places. You can make them into crystallised food decorations by dipping them into egg whites and then fine granulated sugar, before leaving them to dry. They will keep refrigerated in an airtight container for a couple of weeks.

Weather....

You'll notice that the weather starts to get a little warmer and the days a little longer in March. That's because the sun is moving closer to the equator. Towards the end of the month, we have the Spring Equinox, when the day is the same length as the night. At around this time, we also set our clocks forward an hour.

Did you know the full moon in March is called the Worm Moon? This is because lots of plants, animals and insects — including worms — are beginning to re-emerge after winter.

March is a great time to look at Venus. It is the brightest planet and very close to our moon, so it's easy to spot. In March, it's said the planets Jupiter and Venus 'kiss', because you can see them side by side in the sky. To spot them, look west 30 minutes after sunset. As the month goes on, they separate; each night, Venus climbs higher and Jupiter sinks a bit lower.

It is also a great month for spotting the star constellation Draco. The cosmic dragon writhes between the Great Bear (Ursa Major) and the Little Bear (Ursa Minor) in the northern part of the sky. The constellation Draco was named after a dragon that was slain by Hercules in Greek mythology.

Find inspiration in other CELEBRATIONS

With new mothers everywhere in nature, it is perhaps fitting that we usually celebrate Mother's Day at the end of March or the beginning of April. Mums love to be cooked for, so why not try to make her one of our delicious recipes or treat her to a special afternoon tea (see page 30)?

And don't forget about World Book Day! This is a day we celebrate our favourite writers and stories. You could get the whole family involved — dress up as a favourite book character and camp out in the lounge under duvets to read stories by torchlight.

CAMP BESTIVAL HEAD HONCHO & FATHER OF FOUR SONS *Rob da Bank*

HOW TO HAVE EASIER FAMILY ADVENTURES

LET THE KIDS DECIDE

Flip 'the rules' on their heads and have the young people tell the older people what the plan is. I'm still learning the limits of what kids want to do, and don't mind admitting that I still get it wrong, so why not let them make the decision? That way, if it all goes wrong, they can't blame you … but they probably still will!

KEEP IT SIMPLE

Most children and (even occasionally teenagers, if you're lucky) just want to hang out with their parents or carers doing something … anything. I'm definitely guilty of trying to overplan and fill every minute of every adventure, which can result in near-catastrophic errors of timing and a great plan going to pot, very possibly rounded off with a feisty family argument. For the record, I've booked flights on the wrong day and knocked the exhaust pipe off the campervan on the first day of a road trip, while Eli's broken his collarbone on the first day of a holiday — and we still managed to put a smile on our faces and work it out. So keep it simple, plan it well, but don't try to do too much.

BE FLEXIBLE

If you plan a day at the beach and it starts raining, don't just get dejected, pack up and tell the kids the day is ruined. Instead, grab some coats and go rock-pooling, see who can make sand animals with the wet sand, or go swimming in the rain. It might be the best day you've ever had.

LET THE KIDS BRING A FRIEND

Sullen teens can suddenly turn into the funnest, liveliest young people around if they have a mate they can relate to, and younger children can play for hours and hours with a friend in their own magical made-up world. Don't feel guilty that you're not the one they're playing with. After all, you created this wonderful day, so maybe just sit back and enjoy it.

Let's Make

PERFORMANCE MAKE-UP

KIT BAG:

foundation

blending sponge (if you have one)

eyeshadow palette

eyeshadow blending brush (one with a stiffer end to apply colour and a softer end to blend)

eyeliner

eyelash curler (if you have one)

mascara

blusher

Vaseline

angled brush

face-paint in one colour (we use Snazaroo)

cotton bud

glitter

neutral-coloured lip gloss

Isadora, Cirque Bijou

Cirque Bijou have been making surprising circus and street-theatre spectacles for us for a decade — we love the vision, bright and wacky ideas and attention to detail that they bring to Camp Bestival.

Whether making pop-up performances for Caravanserai (Cirque Bijou's performance space at Camp Bestival), bringing together an eclectic mix of artists for a magical parade or creating a spectacular finale show above our audience's heads, Cirque Bijou like to make sure that their work is unforgettable and tailored to the Camp Bestival crowds. Every element is important, from the technical challenges of making pianos fly alongside aerialists, to the detail of getting the costumes and the make-up just right.

They work with large and brilliant teams of specialist artists and show-makers, who all bring their uniqueness to the festival. One of them is aerialist Isadora. She did what some kids dream of. 'I actually ran away to join the circus!' she says. 'My act involves performing acrobatic tricks really high in the sky on a big metal hoop with another performer. Together, we hang upside down, spin really fast and even do the splits! I have travelled all around the country, wearing beautiful costumes and make-up, performing for audiences at festivals like this one.'

Here, Isadora gives you a little insight into the type of make-up that the performers wear. Have a go, follow the steps and you too could become a professional circus artist — even if just for one day.

1. Moisturise and apply a light base of skin-coloured foundation to your entire face using a blending sponge (if you have one), taking care to blend it evenly around the eye creases.

2. Using an eyeshadow blending brush, load the stiffer end with your chosen colour (we used red) and apply shadow from your upper lash line to the eye socket crease. Then use the softer end to blend it around the eye socket crease.

3. Load a pearlised version of your main eyeshadow colour on to a small, stiff brush. You can use two tones of any colour, e.g. blue and pearlised blue, or green and pearlised green. Pat this colour around the tear duct in a 'v' shape and continue out towards the outer corner of each eye. This gives depth. Now apply a bit of this colour to your lower lash line, going from the outer corner towards the tear duct.

4. With a fine eyeliner, draw along your upper lash line, starting from above your pupil and moving outward, finishing with a 'flick' out towards your eyebrow.

5. Use an eyelash curler (if you have one) to curl your lashes, then apply mascara.

6. With an angled brush, using a creamy blusher or powder, draw a crescent shape from the top of your brow to your cheekbones.

7. Enhance your eyebrows using a small amount of eyeshadow in a shade that matches them, and set with a slick of Vaseline.

8. If you would like to draw circus 'diamonds', get an angled brush, wet it and load it with face paint in any colour you like. Draw outlines of the triangles first – one pointing up, and one pointing down. Fill them in and add dots if you wish. You don't have to have symmetry. One big triangle and one small one is OK. If you prefer symmetry, start small so you can adjust them to match if needed.

9. If you would like to add glitter, dot Vaseline on the area where you wish to apply it using a cotton bud, then apply the glitter with your fingers or a sponge applicator.

10. Add a neutral lip gloss that won't 'fight' with the eye colour.

11. Et voilà! You are ready for your performance.

FAMILY FEAST: AFTERNOON TEA @ THE CIRCUS

A high tea is a very easy thing to make look beautiful and exciting. You can create many layers and mix up finger sandwiches, shop-bought items and homemade cakes with colourful icing. The trick is to mix and match the cutlery, crockery and glassware, and go back in time — or perhaps even into the future! Have fun — there are no rules! We originally sourced this crockery with our friend Krista on the Isle of Wight for our 50th birthdays, and it was too good not to reuse it for this shoot. It proves you don't have to spend a fortune to make your hight tea table look special.

We did this shoot to celebrate the Cirque Bijou's 'Circus Café' show, which has happened every afternoon at Camp Bestival for the last ten years. Our friend Billy wrote the sketch a decade ago and each year circus students perform it. We always try to go and watch it as a family — it's very funny and the circus skills are off the scale.

The festival's fabulous Dave the Baker not only made these delicious treats, but also cooked up these fine words of advice:

'High teas have always been a decadent display of leisure and gluttony in miniature. If you plan to smother your guests with all the trappings of deliciousness, then keep the bites small, leave them wanting more. This will keep the mouth free to gossip about the latest society scandal. Perhaps a lady and her groomsman accidentally touched hands at the harvest festival? Or maybe a small dog was elected to the House of Commons? Make the execution easy by choosing a few things that can be made the day before, and balance them with some fresh elements to electrify the taste buds.'

Dave agrees that it's perfectly acceptable to mix homemade with shop-bought. Remember, it's a culinary circus show, and should be full of surprise and spectacle. So, get creative; set a beautiful table, dress up, and try making Dave's delicious flapjacks (see page 204) for an extra-special touch.

APRIL
did you know......

that April comes from the Latin word *aperio*, meaning 'to open'? This is because so many flowers, buds and leaves will unfold in the coming weeks.

≫ get into nature ≪

Have you heard the cuckoo yet? Or seen the swallows return from Africa? If you have, you know that summer is just around the corner, and now is a good time to plant seeds. Radish and tomato seeds are easy to grow on your windowsill. Or, if you have an outside area, why not try growing potatoes in large pots or in the ground?

April is also a good month to spot blossom. You can see the small white flowers of hawthorn, plums and pears in hedgerows, gardens and orchards. And later in the month you will start to see the larger pink flowers of cherry and apple trees too. On quiet days, listen for the bees buzzing between them and watch for birds feeding their young. On sunny days, you may even see slow worms sunbathing on walls or rocks.

FORAGING

Wild garlic is delicious and easy to spot. It has broad leaves and a strong garlic smell but a mild taste. It grows in big clusters on the ground in damp woodland and by shaded hedgerows. Use it instead of basil to make pesto or chop the leaves and mix them into butter to make garlic bread. You can also use the leaves and white flowers in salads.

WEATHER

There is an old saying that 'April showers bring May flowers', because April brings warm sunshine and showers. Perfect weather for plants to grow!

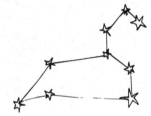

April's full moon is called the Seed Moon. This is because it is the time of birth and growth in nature, and it is a good time to plant seeds.

Close to the Great Bear and Venus is the constellation of Leo, the crouching lion. The story goes that the ancient hero Hercules slaughtered a fearsome lion as the first of 12 tasks to earn forgiveness for a terrible crime. Leo's brightest star, Regulus, is one of the brightest stars in our sky. See if you can spot it: it's the lion's 'front paw', below his head, which is shaped a bit like a back-to-front question mark.

If you go stargazing around the time of the full moon, you might also see the Lyrid meteor showers.

Find inspiration in Other celebrations

In Japan, they have an ancient tradition call Hanami, the Cherry Tree Festival. Parties begin when the cherry trees blossom and end when the petals fall. This means the whole country watches the trees with great excitement.

In Thailand, they wash away the old year with a giant water fight called Songkran. It can last for days and everyone joins in! (Make sure you ask your parents before you celebrate this event!)

The return of spring is celebrated around the world. Eggs are often given as a symbol of new beginnings. This month, we celebrate Easter with the giving — and sometimes rolling — of eggs. If you like, you can use the hedgerow headdress on page 42 as a wreath to welcome in Easter. Or, if you prefer, make it next month and use it as a crown to name yourself Queen of May.

Fearne Cotton

Robby and Fearne have been
mates since their good old days
working together on Radio 1.
They share a love of cold-water
swimming, gong baths and Dorset.
Fearne has also been a regular
guest at Camp Bestival, whether
she's just enjoying the show with
her family or doing a cheeky
Q & A with Robby about how to
parent at the same time as doing
a million other things. Here are
her tips for staying cool when
throwing a party.

HOW TO LESSEN STRESS WHEN THROWING A PARTY

REMEMBER IT'S ALL ABOUT THE PEOPLE

Your guests will enjoy the party due to conversation, proper human connection and a good laugh, not because you've spent five hours tying paper streamers to every surface in your home. They won't care what brand of crisps you put in a bowl, or what kind of gin you're serving. A good party simply requires good people.

ZOOM OUT

When you feel overwhelmed, do what I like to call 'the zoom-out'. Picture yourself in your kitchen, then imagining zooming out so you can see the roof of your home. Then zoom out further to see the area you live in as a small dot in the UK, then again until you see the whole globe, then the universe. Finally, zoom out still further to see the universe as a tiny dot in the infinite expanse of space. This always helps bring perspective.

MAKE A PLAYLIST OF SONGS THAT MAKE YOU FEEL HAPPY

Music always lifts the mood and will pull your focus towards the atmosphere and away from the tiny details.

BE KIND TO YOURSELF

If you're feeling anxious, remember that you're doing great. Hosting a party can cause anxiety as we worry too much about what others might think. We then start to second-guess ourselves and anticipate the worst-case scenario rather than the best outcome. Go easy on yourself.

SET BOUNDARIES THAT WORK FOR YOU

If you don't want kids at your party, or don't want to serve alcohol for personal reasons, then state that clearly. It's your party, so you set the boundaries.

TRY AND ENJOY IT IN THE MOMENT

Sometimes I can feel myself getting stressed about the amount of washing-up I'll have to do afterwards, or whether the carpet on the stairs is getting trashed. Just try and be in the moment and enjoy the party.

MAKE+CREATE

HEDGEROW HEADDRESS

YOU WILL NEED:

**2 × 50cm willow wands (or an alternative, such as
soft ivy creepers)**

**responsibly sourced foliage (from your own garden,
a friend or neighbour's garden (with permission!) or
foraged sparingly, taking only a bit from each plant)**

Spinney Hollow

Spinney Hollow is a place — a ten-acre area of ancient woodland — but it's also a way of life. It's been a staple at Camp Bestival for ten years. The team prides themselves on their 'mix of hobbit and wizard', meaning mixing proper heritage craftsmanship with a large pinch of playful magic, all while keeping a sparkly eye on the importance of imagination and creative stimulation.

It began with just three wood workers, a hazel spider sculpture and, of course, their brown bowtop wagon. Each year, Spinney Hollow grew. Each year they would add something new. Each year, we would say 'yes'. And that allowed Spinney Hollow to experiment and grow. More friends and crafts folk came to help, and the project evolved organically into what it is today. In 2023, Spinney Hollow took up an entire field that housed 200 crew spanning generations and reflecting our family values.

They offer simple activities as well as challenging projects to suit all abilities and ages. Willow-weaving is an incredible way to start the craft journey. For years, the Spinney Hollow team have run the hedgerow headdress workshops in the shade of the brown bowtop wagon — the same wagon they began their Camp Bestival journey with. Making a hedgerow headdress is a great way to learn one of the basics of willow work: weaving a willow hoop. From this hoop, so much is possible, from headdresses and seasonal wreaths to bird feeders and sculptures. Spinney Hollow pride themselves on using materials that can be easily foraged and found.

Jenny has been working with Spinney Hollow since the beginning. She is a marvel of rustic elegance and style, and some of her creations are just incredible! As one visitor said to her, 'I love it here — this is the best bit of the festival! I could sit here and do this all day. It's so therapeutic. Such a chilled and welcoming vibe.'

So, grab the stuff you need, put on some relaxing music, and begin …

1. Bruise or massage the willow wands by gently bending sequential sections of each wand from one end to the other. This makes the wands more supple and less likely to snap, so they are easier to manipulate into a circle.

2. Once soft, twist the two wands together along their full length. It may help to place a foot on one end of the wands so both your hands are free to twist. Tie into a granny knot.

3. Put the hoop on to your head (as you'd like to wear it), and then put your hand inside the loop so that you have a gap of about an inch. You need the hoop to be slightly too big, because the foliage will make it smaller, so this is important. When you're happy with the size, twist any excess bits of willow around the hoop.

4. Select your base foliage. Long, leafy lengths are best. Tuck the thick ends in between the willow twists (you may need to open the weave slightly). Wrap the lengths around the hoop and secure the other end into the hoop in the same way, or wrap it around, depending on the foliage type. Repeat and build up with a variety of types of foliage.

5. Keep trying on the headdress to check the size and fit, and use your hands to keep shaping it to your head and to encourage softness.

6. Natural imperfections are good, as is some asymmetry. Try building up one area more than others, or introducing a pop of colour, dried flowers or a feather for a point of interest.

Note: Ivy is poisonous and can cause skin irritation so take care and always wash your hands after handling.

Tip: Introduce scented flowers, leaves or herbs, such as jasmine, eucalyptus or rosemary.

MAY
did you know......

that May is named after the Greek goddess Maia? She had a son, Hermes, with the god Zeus. As she is an earth goddess and a goddess of growth, we can easily see her connection to spring.

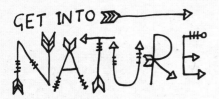

GET INTO NATURE

May is the most beautiful month for wildflowers in the UK. They cram into verges and stone walls, carpet woodland floors and fields and climb hedges. There are pink campions, cow parsley, buttercups and clover. It's also usually the best time to see bluebells, so why not plan a trip to an old woodland to see them in all their glory?

WHAT ELSE?

There are so many flowers at this time of year and all these flowers mean more insects. You may see some large, noisy bugs buzzing around in the evenings. These are probably Maybugs or cockchafers (yes, really), which look like flying furry beetles. May is also a good time to look for moths as they gather around outside lights at night. If you go down to a river or stream, you may spot mayflies as they emerge from the water in their hundreds, with their delicate wings and three 'tails'. Did you know that they only live for a few hours in this adult form?

FORAGING

Clover and hawthorn 'May' flowers are delicious in salads.

Elderflowers will be at their best towards the end of the month, and can be used to make an easy elderflower cordial. Look for elder trees in hedgerows and verges between fields, and in parks or green spaces. Fill a small bucket with flowers on a warm, dry day (you'll need about 20 heads). Gently shake off any bugs. Combine 1kg of white sugar with 1.5 litres of boiled water in a large pan and stir until the sugar dissolves. Add the grated zest and juice of 3 lemons, followed by the elderflower heads. Cover the pan and leave for two days, then strain and bottle. Keep refrigerated and use within two weeks. The cordial is delicious mixed with water, or it can be used as syrup over ice cream, on cakes and in cocktails! Why not make some as a gift for your friends and family?

WEATHER

After April's showers, May is usually sunny and warm. Have you noticed that the evenings are warmer and the days are still getting longer?

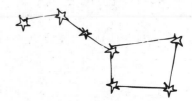

May's full moon is called the Flower Moon or Milk Moon, because flowers are everywhere and all the animals are feeding their young. The Anglo-Saxons called May the 'three milking' month, because their cows could be milked three times a day!

We briefly talked about Ursa Major, the Great Bear, on page 10, but we haven't taken a really good look at it yet, so let's do that now. This is the largest constellation in the northern half of our skies. His head faces east; see if you can spot the seven brightest stars, which form his body and tail. These are known as the Big Dipper, the Plough or the Saucepan. Mizar is the second star from the end of the 'handle'. Look closely at this star. On a dark night, good eyes can see that it is actually two stars close together. Did you know that they used to test a soldier's eyesight like this?

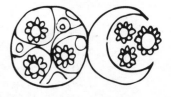

Note: NEVER eat the leaves or bark of the elder tree, as they are poisonous.

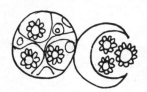

Find Inspiration in other Celebrations

By May, everyone seems to be quite giddy with spring; it used to be the month for falling in love before February stole that particular crown.

Beltane was the first festival to mark this halfway point between the Spring Equinox and the Summer Solstice. Fires were lit to bring back the power of the sun and banish the dark days of winter, making way for new life. Later celebrations introduced dancing and the embracing of topsy-turvy rules, when ordinary folk could be chosen to be 'Lord and Lady' for the day, a tradition that eventually became the crowning of the May Queen.

In Cornwall, they celebrate Flora Day and 'Obby 'Oss at this time. Is there a May Day tradition near you? If not, make yourself a floral headdress like the one on page 42 and crown yourself queen for the day. Don't forget to make up your own rules! You could declare that the family must start the day outside with a fire and a bowl of our Firepit Porridge (page 58). Or you could have it for lunch — you make the rules!

Mike Cuban

Mike Keat, aka Mike Cuban, aka Miguel Mantovani, aka about 200 other made-up characters, is, as you can tell, a man of many faces. Josie and I met Mike in the early 2000s and immediately fell in love with this big-hearted Scotsman who likes pretending to be a Cuban, is a whizz at breakdancing on his head, and can't get enough of funk and soul, good times and making people feel happy and loved. Mike heads up the inimitable Cuban Brothers act, who have played all over the world and, most importantly, haven't missed a Camp Bestival yet. He sang at our wedding and our 50th birthdays, and I imagine we'll be together till infinity! Here's what Mike has to say about music and performing.

HOW TO MAKE IT IN THE MUSIC INDUSTRY

STAGECRAFT

This is all about crowd engagement for me: giving the audience a laugh and sharing with them the other elements I love. It's music driven, but with an element of dance and comedy. It's all about how the audience feel. There's a saying: 'You'll be remembered not for what you've done, but how you've made people feel.' I can relate to that, and that's always the case for me. I make sure the audience have a good time. You have to make an audience feel better than they did when they came in: more relaxed, happier. Your confidence is a big part of this, and will not be mistaken for arrogance. Look them in the eye and connect with them through a bit of banter.

TEAMWORK

When you're performing somewhere, teamwork is very important. Remember it's about the whole team at an event … a team is made up of equal parts, and you are one of them. People say, 'Be nice on the way up, 'cos you'll see these same cats on the way down.' It might be a cliché, but I believe in being a gentleman. That's how I was brought up. So whether you're at a festival or a gig, it costs nothing to have manners and to be respectful.

LOOKING GOOD

Looking good helps set the vibe and inspires confidence too. If you're in a band, have a look that connects you. Have fun with it. It's an age-old trope, but looking good is important and helps convey the tone. It's part of creating an atmosphere that's filled with love, good music, and enjoying the daftness of characters, of people … that's what I like to do.

GET YOUR FAMILY INVOLVED

We love doing Camp Bestival, a festival which has always had my heart. It's where we first took it to the next level, had fun and enjoyed total freedom. So many generations have a good time together at Camp Bestival, which is amazing. I remember raving and partying with my first child, Bonita, at Camp Bestival 15 years ago. Looking out from the stage, you might see a grandma with her son and two or three grandkids in the audience. It's amazing to see generations dancing together. My three young girls have kept me young with their energy. They understand what I do for a living and they always get a buzz from what I do. They don't come to many performances, but they always support me. They've been instrumental in keeping me on the straight and narrow. They keep me in check.

HAVING A THICK SKIN

I'm actually quite a sensitive soul, which might not be obvious from the outside, but one or two negative comments from a gig will stay with me forever. That's just how I am, but the truth is you need to be able to take it on the chin and stay true to yourself — that's entertainment!

BE PREPARED

Consider the words of my friend Woody: 'Remember the five Ps — Perfect Preparation Prevents Piss-poor Performance.'

You're ready.

MAKE+CREATE

MAKE+CREATE
MAKE+CREATE

JUGGLING BALLS

Lucas Jet, Bigtopmania

YOU WILL NEED:

3 sandwich bags

3 cups of rice

9 balloons (ideally 3 of one colour and 6 of another)

Lucas: I was there from the start, and have never missed a Camp Bestival. I even missed my university graduation to be at Camp Bestival, and instead held a mock graduation in its inflatable church. I proposed to my wife during a Fatboy Slim headline set, surrounded by all our nearest and dearest — with accompanying visuals from Norman, thanks to the wider Camp Bestival family.

Camp Bestival crowds are some of my favourite. Families pack into our big top and return year on year to watch us in the Bigtopmania circus show. You can hear them tell first-timers, 'If you see one thing, make sure you go to Bigtopmania'. In a festival with so much on offer, I take that as very high praise indeed. I love teaching circus skills to families, especially when they come back the next year a foot taller and show me their diabolo tricks.

Try making these easy juggling balls, and come and show me your skills next year!

1. Measure one cup of rice into each of the sandwich bags. Twist the top of each one and fold the excess back down around the rice.

2. Snip the end off one of the balloons and place a rice bag inside it.

3. Take a second balloon of the same colour and snip off the end. Put the rice bag in a balloon into this second balloon from the other direction, so that the 'open' end goes in first and covers the hole.

4. Take a different-coloured balloon. Snip off the end and cut three circular holes in the balloon at random places.

5. Stretch this over the double-bagged rice ball. This should give you a multi-coloured ball.

6. Repeat these steps twice, so you have three juggling balls.

JUGGLING TIPS:

- Throw one ball from your left hand to your right hand in a rainbow-shaped arch that peaks at head height. Practise throwing it back and forth, left to right and right to left.

- Take one ball in each hand. Throw the first ball, and when it reaches that central head height, throw the second ball in the opposite direction, so that you catch each ball in the opposite hand to the one with which you threw it.

- Place two balls in your dominant hand (i.e. if you are right-handed, place two balls in your right hand). Place the third ball in your other hand. Throw one ball from the dominant hand and, when it is at head height, throw the ball in the other hand in the other direction (and catch the first ball). When the second ball is at head height, throw the third ball. AND REPEAT.

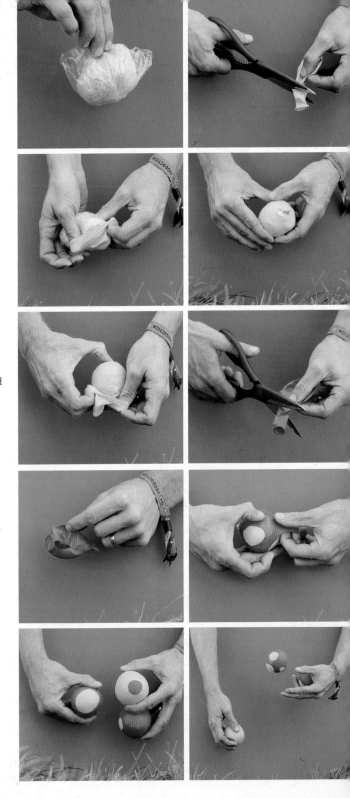

PORRIDGE
with THE BREADUCATOR

Dave the Baker (also known as 'the Breaducator') is the most talented baker out there. He has been part of the Camp Bestival family since the beginning, always in and around the Feast Collective. One day, we hope that he can create his own 'school of bread' on the festival site so you can all appreciate his passion for baking and the simple pleasure it brings.

Dave: I remember it well, that first Camp Bestival. I was coerced into attending by my great friends, who ran Gideon Reeling. I was in my mid-twenties, and the idea of larking about at a kids' festival sounded fun. I think I've only missed two or three since then, and it has been such a huge part of my life. I've done pretty much everything, from performing in the Dingly Dell dressed as a sheep to compèring the Literary Stage, setting up a bakery on site, selling brownies and barbecuing whole beef legs with my mate DJ BBQ and crew. I've run up a pretty big tab, too: countless lifelong friends, a published book of my own, plus more. I hope one day I'll get to repay Rob and Josie for these riches, and I'm sure the line of people who, like me, have been blessed by this beautiful festival is a long one. My most treasured memory has to be watching the Blue Coats, dressed as various sexually transmitted diseases, chasing small, screaming children, while their parents were rendered immobile by fits of laughter. The shouts of 'Gonorrhoea gonna get ya' still ring in my ears.

But here's one of Camp Bestival's more wholesome exports: firepit porridge.

1. When the barbecue is at cooking temperature (smokeless with white embers), barbecue the banana, skin on, on the grill. Alternatively, you can wait until the barbecue is cooling and put the banana directly into the embers. Turn and remove when just blackened on either side. (If you're using soft fruits as an extra topping, you can roast them on the grill at the same time, or you can pan-fry them in butter or maple syrup until golden if you prefer.)

2. Pour the milk into a bowl or jug and place 2–3 hot charcoals into the milk. Depending on how smoky you want the flavour, leave it to infuse for anything from 5 minutes to overnight. Strain the milk through a fine sieve to remove the charcoal. (For a more luxurious version, infuse double cream with charcoal at the same time to use later.)

3. In a saucepan, combine the porridge oats with a pinch of salt and the banana flesh. Add the infused milk and cook over a low heat for around 5 minutes, stirring regularly, until you have a porridge consistency.

4. Melt the butter in a small saucepan over a medium heat for around 5 minutes until browned, taking care not to let it burn. Mix this into the porridge.

5. If you're using seeds as an extra topping, you can use the small saucepan to toast them over a medium heat for 1-2 minutes until golden, then set aside.

6. If you're using infused cream, strain it to remove the charcoal once cold, then whip it into an equal amount of natural yogurt.

7. Divide the porridge between bowls and top with any extra toppings you've prepared.

SERVES 4

FOR THE PORRIDGE:

1 banana
475ml whole milk
300g porridge oats
25g butter
salt

TOPPING IDEAS:

soft fruits, such as peaches
    and nectarines
double cream
natural yogurt
maple syrup
seeds (any mix),
    to decorate

You will also need wood charcoal (not briquettes)

Dave the Baker

Summer is usually associated with
holidays, but having chosen to do what
we do for a living, it's actually our busiest
time of year! We were born a day apart, on
Midsummer's Eve and Midsummer's Day,
so we kick off our summer with a big party
and keep it going all season long with a mix
of celebrations, hastily snatched family time
and a lot of days and balmy nights spent in
a field building festivals. We wouldn't have
it any other way, though — it's a dream job.

June
did you know.......

that June is named after Juno, the Roman Queen of Heaven? It does look like the queen of all months, with its natural beauty and golden midsummer light.

Do you know the difference between a grasshopper and a cricket? Grasshoppers 'sing' during the day by rubbing their hind legs against their wings, while crickets 'sing' at dusk by rubbing their wings together. There are lots of different kinds and they all make different noises. When you are near long grass, see if you can hear them and try to identify different songs.

WHAT ELSE?

June is a good time to spot wild orchids, bats and frogs. Bats come out when the sun goes down — they are most easily seen swooping around, chasing insects at dusk. The tadpoles that hatched in early spring are now insect-eating baby toads or frogs. Late evening, or after heavy rain, is a good time to spot them, as they clamber out of the water to find homes elsewhere.

FORAGING

June is a magical month of long evenings, perfect for foraging walks after school.

Elderflower is one of nature's best medicines. You may already have made elderflower cordial (page 48), but now is the time to gather more flower heads and dry them for future use, as they make a great tea that is said to aid sleep and digestion. You can also use them to make elderflower honey, a herbal cold and flu treatment. Simply crush and chop half a jar of flower heads, then cover to the top with honey. Store in a dark, dry place, stirring daily for the first two weeks. It's ready to use almost immediately, but keeping the flower heads in the honey for longer will strengthen its flavour.

Edible flowers such as dog roses, honeysuckle and dandelion heads taste delicious and can be used in salads or as edible decorations on cakes, puddings and ice cream. Add them to whatever you like for a slightly fruity flavour and maximum gorgeousness.

The Summer Solstice occurs around 21 June, when the Earth's tilt towards the sun is at its maximum. The sun is at its highest and most northerly point in the sky, so we see the longest daylight hours. In fact, sometimes it doesn't get properly dark at all! This is because the sun doesn't set as low in the summer so can produce 'night-shining' clouds.

June's full moon is called the Strawberry Moon. Sadly, its name doesn't come from its colour but from the strawberry harvest this month.

June is good month to spot the southern constellation of Scorpius as it becomes visible north of the equator. You can just see it poking above the horizon if you look south in the late evening. At its heart is a red twinkling star called Antares. Antares represents the heart of Scorpius, the scorpion that killed the great hunter Orion. The gods placed both in the sky but at opposite sides, so as Orion sets, Scorpius rises.

Note: NEVER eat the leaves or bark of the elder tree as they are poisonous.

FiND inspiration from other Celebrations ☆

Thousands of years ago, midsummer's longest day was celebrated as the coming together of heaven and earth, light and dark. That is why in England, pagans still flock to Stonehenge to watch the sun rise or set. In Brawby, Yorkshire, however, they prefer to bake giant Yorkshire puddings for a midsummer boat race. Don't worry, though — they're not daft. They coat the bottoms with yacht vanish first so they don't go soggy!

For many of the world's northernmost countries, which have long, dark winters, midsummer (Midsommar) is a very important festival. In Finland and Sweden, it is traditionally linked to fertility rituals, and is a popular day to get married, light bonfires and eat pickled herring with strawberries. Did you know that these regions have 'white nights' when it doesn't get fully dark, and that in some places it's possible to ski under a midnight sun?

AND DON'T FORGET…

If you celebrate Father's Day this month (but don't like herring), why not make your dad some s'mores (page 76)? They are so easy and fun to make — and taste delicious, too!

Chops & DJBBQ

These guys are barbecuing royalty, known all across the globe and famous not only for being able to make any joint of meat into something super delicious, but also for dressing flamboyantly, rocking Spandex like no one else, and blasting out the best rock 'n' roll anthems. And don't even dare miss Chops and his air guitar when they take to the stage at Camp B for some light relief from all the gnawing on bones and smoke in the eyes. Here, they share how they make the magic.

CHOPS'S PREP PLAYLIST:
Carly Rae Jepsen – 'Call Me Maybe'
Karrion – 'Cider Pirates'
AC/DC – 'It's a Long Way to the Top'
Aerosmith – 'I Don't Want to Miss a Thing'

DJ BBQ'S COOKING PLAYLIST:
Patrice Rushen – 'Haven't You Heard'
**Sister Sledge (Dimitri From Paris remix) –
  'Thinking of You'**
**Pastor TL Barrett and the Youth for Christ Choir –
  'Nobody Knows'**

HOW TO MAKE A BBQ MORE MEMORABLE

DJ BBQ: My biggest tip is this: don't just put charcoal everywhere. Use the half-and-half technique, where you spread out the coals into two piles. Get yourself set up for indirect cooking with different temperature zones; this will cook your food properly to the right temperature. If it gets too hot over on one side of the barbecue, just move the food. Working with fire is always a memorable experience, and this technique will help you cook better. Also, maybe make more things yourself, like the breads.

Chops: Why buy in bread when you can make it? It's really simple, and you can get your kids involved. Getting them involved will make it more memorable. You can make a simple bread dough, or even a yogurt and flour-based one, a non-risen dough. Get everyone to shape them, and you can even add in herbs and spices for flavour. Then they can just go directly on to the grill to be cooked off. And don't ever make it so there's just one person stuck in the corner manning the barbecue while everyone else is having fun … get everyone to have a go, and get everyone making breads.

DJ BBQ: Our whole ethos with barbecue is cater-tainment. The quickest way to someone's heart is through their stomach — and their ears. Good food and good music equals good times … it's an equation that works! Simple maths with DJ BBQ and Chops! So, get yourself a really good playlist, or maybe choose one of your favourite artists and go to their online playlists and put that on. The other day I went to one of my friend's restaurants, and he just had George Clinton radio on, and it was like the best three hours I've ever had cooking — all this rad funk, and I'm working the smoker, doing wings, making fish tacos and having a blast 'cos the music's right. That's cater-tainment!

DJ BBQ: And try dirty cooking. You only have so much real estate on that grill, so why don't you go into the coals? It's quite empowering to go into the coals, and it's also quite campfire. Throw your onions in there, your beetroots, your potatoes — any kind of root vegetable will work really well. Aubergines work, too. We make a great baba ghanoush by cooking the aubergines in the coals.

Chops: Do barbecues and outdoor cooking more. Bring the indoors outdoors. Cottage pie, lasagne, classic home-cooked meals, any pasta dish — you don't need to cook them indoors. You can use your barbecue. Don't just let it be a summer thing where you all go outside and cook together. Do it all the time, even if you're doing a Moroccan thing, or …

DJ BBQ: A chilli!

Chops: Yes! A chilli is great over the coals. It's a really lovely heat. You can even cook desserts over a barbecue.

DJ BBQ: Just bring it outside!

Chops: Yup, bring it outdoors. It will be more memorable.

DJ BBQ: I don't know why we just cook barbecue in the summer. Who wants to stand around hot coals in the blazing sun? Not us … but Robby and Josie, your festival is at the end of July, so we have to do it — ha ha ha! But the rest of the year, why not barbecue then too? My preferred time to barbecue is through the winter and the early spring. I love it when it's crisp and cold, getting outside and firing up my grill and standing around what is essentially an outdoor heater, ya know? Like Chops says, use that grill 365 … the more you use it, the better you're gonna get at it. And use seasonal produce! We love cooking outside in the winter, and that really works with the holidays and Christmas. You only have so much room in your oven for Christmas dinner, so take the main event outside and you've got more room indoors.

(See page 176 for DJ BBQ and Chops's Turkey on the Grill recipe.)

A WOODLAND FAMILY

YOU WILL NEED:
your outdoor shoes
a grown-up (also useful for reaching high branches)
blue tack
felt-tip pens

To us, Camp Bestival is a whimsical, dreamy little world that sits on top of a rainbow. It's a place where all the senses are celebrated. Somewhere to express, make, create and learn through experiences with people of all ages.

You can find Rhea, Eli, Tao and Zen helping the lovely Camp Bestival team as they colour in the canvas of blank site fields. Rhea is easily spotted as she's 'the grinning girl' walking around covered in paint, singing to herself.

Rhea says: 'I love the nature that Camp Bestival is nestled in, and I especially love the woodland walks, and all the amazing giant trees that are hundreds of years old.'

To celebrate this, join her in making a cute mini acorn family. Why not bring it to Camp Bestival this summer as your mascot?

1.   Go out to a park, the woods, a beach or your garden in search of twigs, leaves, pebbles and shells. If you'd like to try this in September, you can look for acorns and conkers as well.

2.   Bring everything home, get cosy and have fun making — just like we did in the photos! Use the blue tack to make bodies and attach different bits together. Felt-tip pens are useful for drawing faces and other details. We made mushrooms, people, a ladybird, and even an ant on its back. What will you make?

Rhea, Eli, Tao & Zen

family feast

S'MORES

S'mores seem like a very modern, 21st-century thing to middle-aged dads like me. I can't recall exactly when I first heard this strange word, and in fact, I've just had to use a well-known search engine to discover why a s'more is called a s'more. (It's an abbreviation of the phrase 'some more', so there you go … you have to write a book to discover these things sometimes!) Apparently, the first s'more recipe appeared in the Campfire Marshmallow cookbook in the early 1920s — that's 100 years ago, kids!

Our own kids seem to jam anything around a marshmallow and call it a s'more. Marshmallow and chocolate between digestive biscuits or crackers seems like a good start, but you can add or subtract pretty much anything. Ice cream is very tasty with toasted marshmallows, and makes things even messier — which is great!

Miller and I got busy around the campfire at home, and this is what we came up with.

1. Toast a marshmallow on your skewer until completely golden on the outside but not burnt.

2. While your toasted marshmallow is cooling, spread chocolate spread on two biscuits.

3. Sandwich the marshmallow in between the biscuits, with the chocolate spread on the inside. It is good to choose biscuits that are a similar size to the marshmallows, so pair big biscuits with giant marshmallows, and small biscuits with the regular ones.

4. Try not to get marshmallow all over your face.

Tip: You'll need an adult to light the fire and help toast the marshmallows. Wood or charcoal fires are best. It is good to use long skewers. Here, we used metal ones, but wooden skewers or sticks are much better, as they don't get hot! If using a stick, ask an adult to sharpen one end with a knife first.

YOU WILL NEED:
marshmallows (the bigger,
  the better)
chocolate spread
biscuits
skewers

Robby & Miller

JULY

did you Know.......

that July is the birth month of Julius Caesar? And since the time of his treacherous murder, the month has been named after him.

GET INTO NATURE

Step into the warm days of summer. This is the month that young birds of prey learn to hunt for themselves. They live in towns and the countryside, on top of tall buildings and on high ledges. You can sometimes hear them screeching loudly to their parents as they learn to fly and dive. Owlets are also learning to fly at this time, and you might hear them in woods.

Little birds are getting ready to leave home, too. If you have a bird bath, keep it topped up. Or put a shallow dish of water out each day for animals such as hedgehogs, so they can get a much-needed drink during hotter weather.

WHAT ELSE?

Poppies and cornflowers grow in cereal fields and dragonflies dance by water. Flying ants fill the air, and daisies, crickets and grasshoppers carpet the ground. So pretty much anywhere you walk, you are going to find something. Take a break, make a daisy chain and see what you can identify?

FORAGING

Chickweed grows everywhere – in your garden, on wasteland and on verges. But did you know that it has cleansing and healing properties, and is packed full of vitamins and minerals? Look for its small, white star-like flower. Its tender leaves and flowers can be used in salad with a lemon and oil dressing, or blended to make pesto. Alternatively, wilt it in a pan with butter, salt and pepper and serve with fish or chicken.

Chanterelle mushrooms are also well worth finding from July and into autumn. Look for the golden, trumpet-shaped chanterelle in all kinds of woodland, from pine to mixed wood. These mushrooms are delicious served with eggs. The chanterelle's wavy shape distinguishes it from the false chanterelle, which looks and smells more like a typical mushroom (and just happens to be a similar colour). Always double-check you have correctly identified any mushrooms before you eat them.

Wild strawberries really like woodland, hedgerows and rough grassland, so keep an eye out for them as you walk around looking for chickweed and chanterelles. These little berries are small, but mighty in taste.

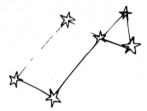

July's full moon is often called the Hay Moon, for fairly obvious reasons. Native Americans called it the Full Buck Moon, because this is the time when antlers appear on young buck deer.

Looking up into the night sky, close to Draco, you will find the constellation of Lyra. It is small but perfectly formed in the shape of the lyre, a musical instrument of Ancient Greece. Vega is its brightest star and the fifth brightest star in the sky. Next to Vega is Epsilon Lyrae, which might look like it's just one star by eye. But if you look through binoculars, it's possible to see up to two stars. And if you look through a telescope you can see up to four. There are at least five stars that make up Epsilon Lyrae, but they're so close together it's easy to mistake it for just one star.

Find Inspiration In Other Celebrations

Anyone for tennis? For those who love tennis, July is all about Wimbledon. For the rest of us, July means strawberries, long school holidays and festivals of all kinds: music, comedy, theatre … and mud!

Yes, that's right — mud. In a month when mud is usually far from our minds, South Korea dedicates a whole festival to it. This is not rooted in an ancient ritual, but it is fun! Festival-goers listen to K-pop and splash, wallow and swim in the special health-giving mud of the region.

Why not make a mud kitchen using Abbie's instructions on page 94 and join in the mud fun? And if you're at Camp Bestival this month, come and see her in her kitchen. She'll love to hear all about the one you made at home!

Ned Abel Smith

Ned is like the court jester of Camp Bestival. Never knowingly underdressed, he loves a good cape or cloak as much as Robby ... possibly more. His endless patience and enthusiasm for not only helping his own kids whittle a wand or start a fire with some sawdust and Vaseline, but also anyone else who happens to be about, is infectious. His is always one of our favourite faces to see, both at Camp Bestival and at home. Here's what he has to say about dressing up and having fun.

HOW TO DRESS UP AND LET GO!

Ned: Camp Bestival is the escape the whole family needs from the crazy noise and distractions of daily life.

The best way to make the outside world fade away fast is to immerse yourselves in the wild and colourful festival environment. You can do this by discovering your inner child, and a great way to do this is … PLAYING DRESS-UP!

Sequins, feathers, crazy leggings, glitter, headdresses, hats and cloaks: these are our 'go-to' ways of stepping into the world of enchantment and joy! Sequins shimmer and dance, giving an instant twinkle and a shot of pizazz. Feathers are flirty and whimsical (go big), glitter makes you shine (go REALLY big), and a cloak (go even BIGGER!) swathes you in mystery, thus completing your transformation …. et voilà! Instantly you are a magician, a fairy, a champion of wit as you step into another world. You are a spirited character in your own journey of excitement and wonder. (Plus, on a practical note, a cloak can offer you total UV protection in the sunny daytime, while at night it acts as a blanket to keep you warm!)

Every year, Camp Bestival has a theme. Disco. Love. Space. It's fun to incorporate this theme into what you wear. Step out of your comfy clothes and dress up — then go off and explore! Enjoy your adventure into the rapturous unknown. Don't be afraid to stray far from your campsite and into the colourful fields, where the flags fly high and the pipers play. Uncover as many secrets as you dare. Meet with the fairy folk while your children build shields and swords, all of you becoming your own mini artisanal clan.

And don't forget the food, glorious food! It's so easy to keep everybody well fed on delicious, wholesome food at Camp Bestival. There are plenty of incredible food stalls to choose from, and the food is an experience in itself, from wild-fired slabs of steak and chimichurri, to warming soups, curries, crêpes, and even the occasionally late-night dirty burger and fries (my wife's fave!). Glorious barbecue scents and spicy aromas fill the air, adding to the sense of magic, rousing your senses and filling your hearts as well as your bellies. You never have to worry about finding great food (or doing the washing-up!).

Music, entertainment and MANDATORY dancing: do all of it! Tumble into your tents feeling full. Full of joy. Full of soul. Full of excitement for tomorrow. Wake up the next day, drink a delicious coffee from one of the many quirky little coffee tents, and repeat ALL of the above. You will find new delights awaiting you when you unzip that flysheet.

Robby and Josie have been putting on music festivals since the dawn of time, so trust me: there will be live acts that the whole family will be buzzing for. There will be dancers to be inspired by, and circus-style performers that will make you gasp in wonder. Extraordinary entertainment that simply wows. AND there's so much of it!

The entire festival zings with creativity. It's a visual feast that ignites the creative spirit within. Even if you aren't used to getting your hands dirty or simply trying something new, you won't be able to resist! So be a kid again, and join in with the children. As a family, we all love to do and make things together at Camp Bestival. From lantern-making, axe-building and headdress-weaving, you can give everything a go! It's a welcoming world full of kind artists who will guide you through all of it.

Camp Bestival is special. Its uniqueness lies in the way it reminds us all of the simple joys of being outside, reconnecting with family or friends, listening to wonderful music, getting creative, sharing fabulous food, and letting your inner child run around and get a bit giddy. All of this brings us closer together, making memories and beautiful moments for everyone to treasure.

Cloak hack: A decent cloak doubles up as an emergency tent for your little nipper should they need a private poo!

BUM BAG

Cheryl Griffiths, Textile Junkies

YOU WILL NEED:

pattern (see page 222)
  fabric (at least 100cm x
  25cm)
26cm zip
25mm wide webbing

25mm side-release plastic
  buckle
thread
sewing machine
iron (optional)

Cheryl: When I was a child, the house was filled with garments to be pinned and fitted, and lots of female chatter. My grandmother was a dressmaker, and so was my mother. Eventually I returned to the fold (after a fling with art school) and brought with me a more flamboyant approach to dressmaking. We cleared a space amongst the wedding dresses and tweed and started making crazy clubwear and fancy dress for the colourful '90s rave scene. And the name of the business? 'The Dressmaker's Daughter', of course.

I was introduced to Camp Bestival by my friend and business partner, Graham Breakwell. He is a regular visitor and agent for Circus Raj and the Grand Indian Bazaar. That first visit took me back to those heady days of the '90s — only this time, the ravers had kids!

It really is a pleasure to watch kids and families making bucket hats and bum bags, just like we did. Some days the queue to get on to a sewing machine can be quite daunting. Everyone wants to make one. There is the odd swear word, but what I remember most are the mothers who say, 'Thank you for what you do.' They get really emotional — especially the ones whose sons get really engaged in the process of sewing. It's such a good skill to encourage.

The funniest thing I've ever made? Probably the brain costume I made for the Welsh government. But I'll make anything — and I'll show anyone how to do it. Through Textile Junkies, my mission is to teach people skills that will enable them to live more sustainably through mindful, creative practice. I want to share my passion for 'slow fashion', something I've been practising since I was a kid … do you think it will catch on?

With these instructions, you can make your own bum bag at home. The instructions may look a bit complicated, but take it slowly and look at the photos to check what you're doing at each stage.

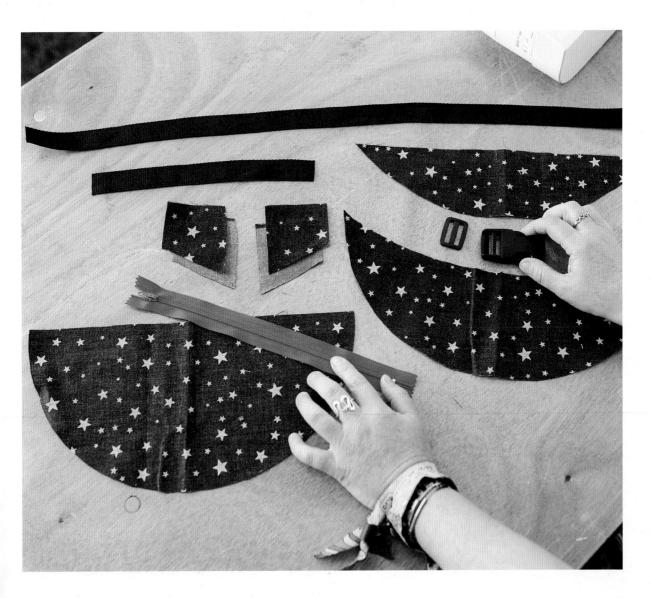

START BY MAKING THE BELT ATTACHMENT

1. Take the four belt attachment pieces, and put the right sides together to make two pairs. Using a sewing machine, sew the top and bottom (diagonal) sides, leaving the two side seams open. Repeat for the other pair.

MAKE UP THE BELT STRAP

1. Thread the short end of the strap through the buckle.

2. Put the long strap length through the slider.

3. Thread the long strap through the buckle and then back through the slider.

4. Seal the ends of the strap by folding over twice and stitching.

5. Insert the short strap ends into the wide end of one of the belt attachment pieces made in step 1. Close the far end with a seam.

6. Repeat for the other side. (Tip: Make sure the strap is parallel to the top seam, not squiffy.)

7. Trim the diagonal corners so that the fabric is not too bulky when you turn it the right way. Now turn the pieces the right way so that the right sides are facing out.

ATTACHING THE BELT TO THE BAG

1. Align the top of the belt attachment with the notch on the back piece and sew together. Repeat with the other side, making sure that the belt strap is not twisted when you insert it.

MAKING THE FRONT

1. Put the upper and lower front pieces together, with right sides facing each other.

2. Sew from the outside corner to the notch only. Repeat on the other side.

INSERTING THE ZIP

1. With the right side facing up, place the zip (with the zip pull facing down) into the gap, aligning the centre of the zip with the centre notch.

2. Pin the lower edge of zip to the lower front edge. (Tip: Make sure the seams are opened out.)

3. Change to the zipper foot on the sewing machine.

4. Open the zip halfway and sew to the middle. Leaving the needle in the fabric, lift up the foot, then close the zip and sew to the end.

5. Repeat on the other side.

MAKING BAG

1. Put the right sides of the front and back bag pieces together (aligning the central notches) and pin.

2. Sew along the top edge.

3. Open the zip.

4. Align the back bottom notch with the front bottom notch. Pin and sew together.

5. Trim the corners (to minimise bulk), then turn the right way. Iron, if you like.

family feast
MUD KITCHEN FUN

Abbie organises the Dingly Dell area at Camp Bestival, which is home to 'messy play', clay workshops, and our infamous Mud Kitchen. Abbie is one of our favourite members of staff, as she doesn't mind getting down and dirty and stuck in with the kids, whether she's helping build the show with Josie or lending a hand in the Mud Kitchen over the weekend when it's overrun with beautiful, young and very muddy children! Here's her guide to the ultimate mud kitchen 'feast'.

Abbie: I'm part of Camp Bestival's creative crew. The mud kitchens that we build are always popular with the younger ones — and sometimes the adults, too! They're an excellent way for kids to cook up a fantasy meal and get wonderfully muddy at the same time.

They really can be made from any old thing. Do you have an unused wooden pallet kicking about? If so, chop it up and piece together something that resembles a table. Maybe even add a cooking hatch or a pretend café window if you're feeling adventurous. It's a really playful way to create an outdoor space for the kids.

Now, for the feast to commence, you just need to set the scene — and have plenty of mud at the ready.

In true Camp Bestival style, we love to add a touch of colour to our mud kitchens. Bunting made from recycled fabric is a real favourite, along with hand-painted slab-wood signage. Streams of colourful ribbon hanging from trees and large painted lampshades also help to make the area feel like a wonderland.

Reuse old kitchen utensils in your mud kitchen; spoons and mixing bowls are the best for making big mud cakes. For the mud, topsoil creates the smoothest consistency when mixed with water, but compost also works a treat. We like to add little pots of twigs and leaves to our mud café shelves, too.

Your kids now have all the ingredients to create the perfect mud kitchen feast at home. It's so fun to see what they'll make and how adventurous they can be. This is the perfect time for them to immerse themselves in nature and be a little bit wild!

Of course, their muddy concoctions will sound delicious, but they definitely aren't for eating. And we always avoid glass or plastic in the mud kitchen — stick to the un-breakables!

Abbie Gadsden

AUGUST

did you Know......

that the month of August is named after the first Roman emperor Augustus? He chose it because it was his lucky month, and stole a day from February to make it 31 days long (so that it was at least as long as Julius Caesar's 'July').

≫ get into nature ≪

With the sun having warmed it up, August is the time to be on the water, or in it. If you're heading to the coast on your summer holidays, rock pools are among the best things to explore. Head to rocky shorelines at low tide, then dig around the seaweed and gently lift up rocks in the water to see what you can find. Crabs, shrimps, anemones, limpets, snails and starfish can all be seen in rock pools around the coast. Remember to check that you don't get cut off by the tide.

WHAT ELSE?

It's possible to see common dolphins from the beach, but you have more chance of seeing harbour porpoises from a boat. Or, if you are at the beach, why not see what you can spot in rockpools at low tide?

Away from the coast, butterflies gather in warm, sunny spots; look out for chalkhill blues, peacocks, and red admirals. Heather comes into flower at this time, turning moors and heathland purple with its nectar-rich flowers. Meanwhile, swallows begin their long return to Africa. Other migrating birds will follow next month.

FORAGING

August marks the beginning of harvest time, with blackberries, elderberries, cherries and sloes ripening this month.

Crab apples are now ready for picking. These are small brown apples that often grow wild and, because they have high levels of pectin, they can be added to berries (see below) to set jams and jellies.

Blackberries are easy to find, because prickly bramble will grow anywhere that it is allowed to. These dark purple berries are high in vitamin C and can be eaten uncooked or in pies and crumbles. Try to avoid berries growing near busy roads or at dog height, though!

WEATHER

With holidays on our minds and harvests to gather, August weather can seem unpredictable. This is because Britain lies under an area where five main air masses meet; wetter masses come from the Atlantic Ocean, and warm, dry ones from the large land mass of continental Europe.

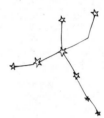

The farmers' name for August's full moon is the Corn Moon because of the harvest, but it's sometimes called the Red Moon because the summer haze can make it look red. Can you see that the moon looks bigger and brighter this month? This is because it is closer to Earth than normal. Occasionally, we have two full moons in August!

The constellation of Cygnus is also large and bright this month. Its cross shape is easy to imagine as a swan flying over the Milky Way. The central star is called Sadr, and from here its head stretches out to Albireo, probably the most beautiful double star in the sky. If you look really hard, you can see its amber and blue lights. Greek mythology says that upon his death, Orpheus the musician was turned into a swan and placed in the sky next to his instrument (the Lyre, which we saw last month on page 80).

PEA
CE O

Find inspiration in other Celebrations

With plenty to pick, gather and eat, August celebrates the beginning of the harvest and the storing of surplus food. Lammas (meaning 'loaf') is the traditional harvest celebration from which most modern harvest festivals stem.

A mass tomato battle between children that started in 1945 in Buñol, Spain, eventually evolved into the festival La Tomatina. During this event, probably the world's messiest food fight, the whole town celebrates the tomato harvest by throwing tomatoes at each other.

Celebrate plentiful fruit and vegetables this month with Ben and Holly's vegetable carving (page 104). This is a useful skill that can be used again in October and December.

Jo Whiley, Broadcaster & DJ

Another Radio 1 alumnus, alongside Robby, Jo has long been a beacon of positive parenting for Robby and Josie as they encounter her out and about at festivals with numerous offspring and hangers-on, not only enjoying the festivities but also very often casually presenting some live TV coverage, interviewing the stars, and looking super glam to boot. What a woman! Here are her tips for getting the most out of your time at a festival.

HOW TO HAVE THE BEST TIME AT A FESTIVAL WITH KIDS OF ALL AGES

*AND NOT KILL EACH OTHER

TAKE FRIENDS

All of you. It will ease the pressure all round. Spending ten minutes whittling knives out of wood is fun. Spending three hours trying to get a spark out of two bits of flint can be a bit much. Far better if you release your charges with their best mate to do what they love while you do what you love. Which I'm guessing will be either watching an alternative comedian making a stream of gags about festival goers or enjoying a 'fine dining' experience (don't even THINK about taking a small person to one of these — you'll be bankrupt and they'll be hungry).

AGREE TO DISAGREE

You might think you all get on brilliantly and sing to the same tune in the kitchen but when you get to a festival there WILL be musical differences. One of you will see that your old favourite band is on the bill and there is no way on earth that your 12/15/21 year old is going to indulge you and go see Ned's Atomic Dustbin or Gay Bikers on Acid. Not going to happen. So you go have your fun with your tribe and let them go enjoy their latest TikTok discovery. As if you'd even be allowed to go with them anyway.

PLAN YOUR OUTFITS WELL IN ADVANCE

Make the most of the opportunity to wear everything in your fancy dress box all at the same time. If you've always wanted to go to a festival dressed as Spider-Man or a Knickerbocker Glory ice cream — the great British festival is where you can do it without any fear of ridicule. You'll be in great company and have the most fun. Fancy dress is liberating and it's something you can all do together. My daughter India dressed up as the Rocketman when the family went to see Elton at Glastonbury. As did about 200 others. They all gravitated towards each other and we have the most brilliant photo of them all together in the aftermath of Elton's set.

IF AT ALL POSSIBLE, GET THERE EARLY AND STAY TILL JUST BEYOND THE BITTER END

Make the most of every available second of your festival. If you get there before it begins when the gates open, you'll have a magical time setting up your pitch and surveying the site coming together. The beautiful calm before the carnival kicks off. If you can, leave the morning after the Sunday night so that you get to enjoy the grand finale and avoid festival FOMO. Accept that you will be in traffic for much of the day and know that Monday will be a write-off. Make a playlist for the return journey, save some snacks so you don't have to join the epic queues at the first service station you see and let the kids sleep. Conversation at this point will be futile and probably impossible.

AND REMEMBER: ALWAYS HANG YOUR TENT OUT TO DRY THE MOMENT YOU GET BACK

No one wants to sleep in a tent smelling of mould.

See you in a field somewhere next year!

MAKE & CREATE

RADISH CARVING

YOU WILL NEED:

- selection of radishes (odd shapes are good)
- fruit, vegetables and/or foliage, for decoration
- cocktail sticks
- carving kit or small craft knife
- small cookie cutters, if you have any

Ben & Holly, Feast Collective

Holly: It was 2016. Josie and I were both pregnant and ended up giving birth in the same hospital at the same time ... and then we were both onsite at Camp Bestival four days later! Ben was hosting cooking demos, running a breakfast club and showing people how to poach eggs — hundreds of eggs — while Robby and Josie ran the show, with our collective children and babies everywhere! Stiches 'n' all.

Looking back, it was madness! But we have a wonderful friendship forged through all our madcap foodie adventures — most of which tend to happen in muddy fields.

Fast-forward a few years, and it was the year of the massive storm. Sideways rain, hurricane winds, tents flying off like the house in *The Wizard of Oz* — all to the soundtrack of A Tribe Called Quest blasting in the background. It was also the year we set up the Grazing Garden. This comprised a shipping container turned coffee bar, and what was supposed to be a small marquee doing pulled pork and bacon sandwiches. But Ben arranged enough staff, equipment and meat to feed the whole site three or four times over. What with the torrential downpours and rivers running down the hills, we had so much left over that we ended up paying for it to go into a deep freeze. That Christmas, we decided to donate it to the Isle of Wight food bank, so it was a happy ending in a way, despite being a rather costly exercise.

Over the years, we've learned a lot of lessons. Trading at festivals is akin to putting money on a really fun horse race — you never know what's going to happen or how it's going to go. The most important thing is to keep it simple! Cooking healthy foods is not only better for your body, but it's also far easier to clean up when you're in a field without proper washing-up facilities. Another favourite lesson of ours is to make food fun. So take a look in your fruit and vegetable basket, grab a craft knife and let's make something.'

This project was inspired by the Mexican 'Night of the Radishes', which happens in December, but you can use any vegetables, pumpkins, or even firm fruit — whatever is available.

1. Decide on your characters and the scene you want to create.

2. Make your shapes in the radishes by peeling off the outside flesh (with the knife) to expose the contrasting white flesh inside. Knives are sharp, so you may need adult help.

3. For detailed areas, draw on the radish first, either with a sharp pencil or one of the cocktail sticks to leave an impression, then carve over the lines. Working from the top down is easiest when peeling off skin.

4. Smaller parts, like arms and legs, can be cut from larger pieces and attached with short lengths of cocktail sticks.

5. Use other fruits, vegetables or foliage to make accessories or scenery. It's also possible to carve letters … if you want to.

festival BREAKFAST with.... MR + Mrs MEARS

Mr and Mrs Mears, as they're affectionately known on the Isle of Wight, are some of our best mates. The family da Bank and the Mears's, including their daughter Tallulah, are often spotted camping together in unusual locations and rustling up some mega feasts on an outdoor firepit. As a scout leader, Mr Mears's is very handy on the grill, and Sam is a master chef in her own right. Tasting this dish was a delight!

Mrs Mears: We started going to Camp Bestival with Christos and Jessica. Our first one was the Mad Hatter's Tea Party. Ah! We so enjoyed the dressing up and karaoke around a campfire! Later, our youngest, Tallulah, joined in, and we haven't missed one since!!

We've camped in tents, campers, even a caravan one year. We'd rather sleep under the stars than miss it! We've dragged many friends and family there over the years. Our highlights include: watching Kool and the Gang with my best friend Eleanor from school; all the dressing up (especially as a 'Flea Circus', which saw a gaggle of us dressed up as fleas and having lots of photos taken while shouting 'Fleeeeeeas!!!'); having my eyebrows glued down for the first time (!); and squirting people with water pistols from behind signs, something which kept us entertained for an entire afternoon. You can get away with much more mischief when you're dressed up! We've also loved watching Level 42, Ed Sheeran, more Kool and the Gang, Groove Armada and All Saints — and you can never miss out on the Cuban Brothers.

No matter the weather, there's always something to entertain you. And the offerings are always evolving, from saunas to roller-skating! I tried yoga for the first time this year with the amazing Laura and loved it so much. I even tried two more classes over the weekend.

Camp cooking is always good fun in a group. We love feeding as many people as possible — sharing is caring at Camp Bestival. Oh, and of course, we love to make cocktails. Rhubarb margaritas are our go-tos, but we also enjoy plenty of Bloody Marys!

But all that fun requires plenty of fuel. Here's how to make pancakes good enough to keep you full of energy for a day of Camp Bestival excitement. I love serving them with fruit. You can either forage for fruit such as blackberries, or buy any fruit you like — blueberries, banana, strawberries … I'm going to try some pineapple rings. I'm thinking pineapple fritter pancakes!

1. The easiest way to make the batter is with friends. Combine all ingredients in a jug and whisk well. Pass it around the fire and let everyone have a go. Get them to add a wish or two — no sneezing, though, please! We make our batter the night before so it's well rested. Otherwise, we recommend leaving it to rest for at least 20 minutes before cooking.

2. Heat the oil or butter in a frying pan over a medium heat, then pour a small ladle of batter into the pan. Add a few pieces of your chosen fruit and cook for 1—2 minutes until small holes start to form on top of the batter. Turn the pancake and cook on the other side for another 1—2 minutes. Repeat with the remaining batter.

3. Serve with extra fruit and/or sauce.

Hope you're all hungry now!!

MAKES 10 PANCAKES

YOU WILL NEED:

220g plain flour

1 tablespoon baking
  powder

pinch of salt

2 large eggs

1 teaspoon caster sugar

1 tablespoon butter, melted

300ml milk (dairy or
  alternative)

vegetable oil/butter,
  for frying

fruit of your choice

jam, maple syrup –
anything you fancy, really!

The Mears Family

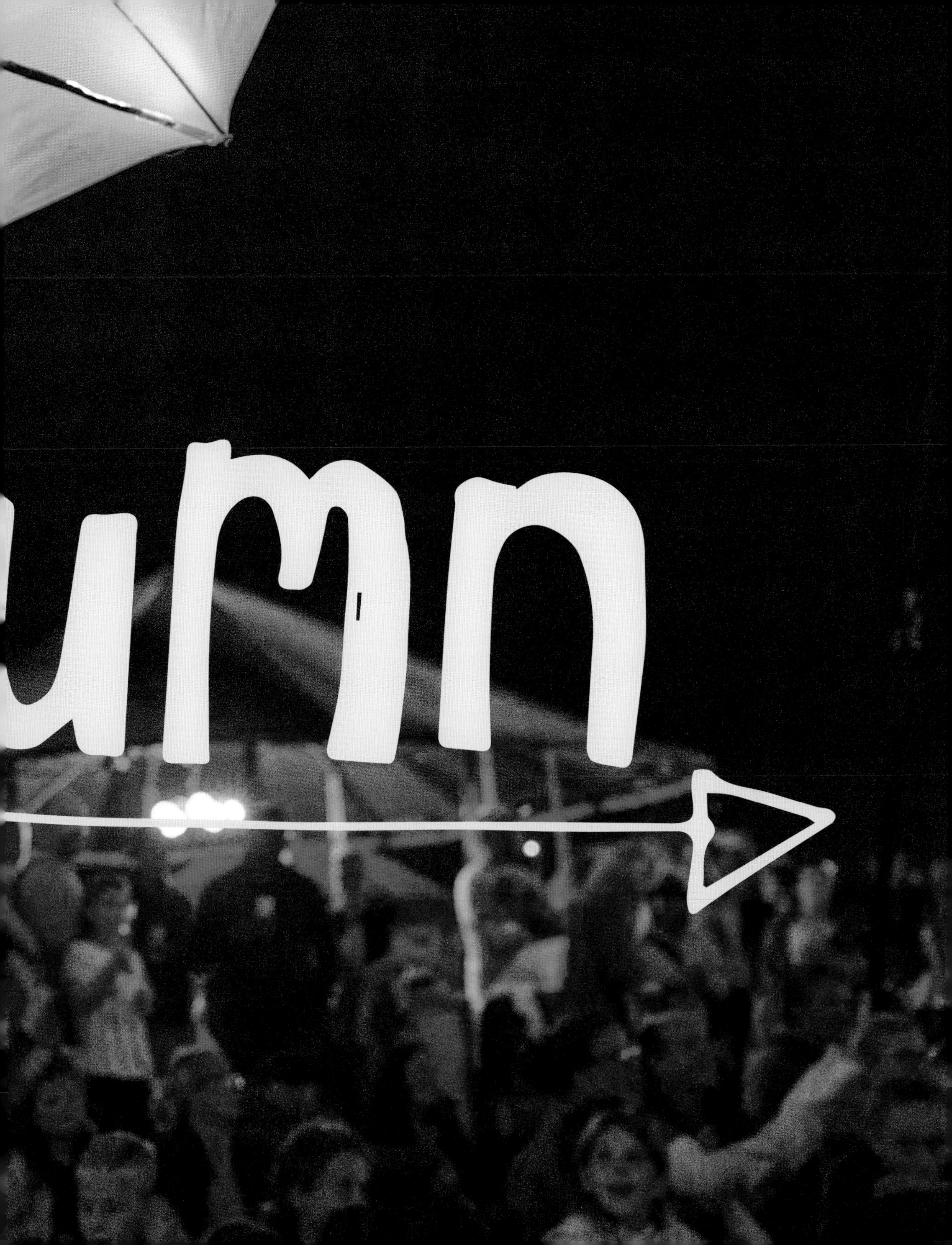
umn

Along with spring, autumn is one of our favourite times of year. This is when we can actually relax a bit after the summer's shenanigans, remember what our kids look like and watch the incredible autumnal colours shift on our island paradise. As keen sea swimmers, this is peak bathing time and a great chance to get back to nature.

September
did you know.......

that the Roman year used to begin in March? This meant that September was the seventh month, or *septem* in Latin.

get into NATURE

September is a time of change and a time of plenty. Leaves are turning brown and garden birds are getting their winter feathers. Summer visitors such as swallows and house martins return to Africa, while birds from Northern Europe and the Arctic fly in. Small mammals, such as hedgehogs, dormice and squirrels, are busy gathering food to prepare for winter, while larger mammals, such as deer and grey seals, are about to enter the breeding season.

WHAT ELSE?

Autumn or winter is a good time to plant trees, but make sure you don't try on a day where the ground is too wet.

At this time of year, you can help small animals find shelter by leaving quiet corners of the garden wild for them to hide in. And why not build a bug hotel? This will provide hidey-holes for all sorts of creatures and can be made from garden waste, such as sticks, leaves, rotten logs, old pallets, cardboard and garden canes.

FORAGING

Berries and nuts cover the hedgerows in September. Gather the last of the blackberries and search for red rosehip berries from wild roses, or dark, round sloe berries from blackthorn trees. Rosehips can be boiled down with sugar and strained to make a sweet, sticky syrup that will keep colds and flu at bay. Your parents may enjoy making sloe gin for the colder months, too! It's so easy.

Field mushrooms are less common now, but are still fairly easily found in grazed fields. Look for white, round mushrooms that flatten out as they grow. They have pink/brown gills (underneath the caps) and go a bit pink if you squish them. Fry them in butter and eat them in omelettes or risotto, with chicken or on toast. Delicious! ALWAYS double-check you have correctly identified any mushrooms before you eat them.

WEATHER

The Autumn Equinox occurs around 23 September and is the second time in the year that the sun is exactly above the equator, meaning that the day and night are the same length. After this date, the sun moves further away, making our days shorter.

September's full moon is called the Harvest Moon. Have you noticed that Jupiter is at its brightest at this time? This is because Jupiter and Earth reach their closest point soon after the Autumn Equinox. Did you know that Jupiter has 79 official moons?

A good constellation to spot this month is Cepheus. It's shaped like a child's drawing of a house, and is visible to the top right of Polaris, the North Star. Cepheus was named after a mythical king of Ethiopia who was married to Queen Cassiopeia. Together with daughter Andromeda, they are part of many gruesome Greek myths.

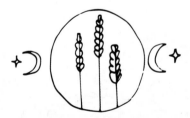

Find Inspiration in other Celebrations

There are a few big festivals worldwide this month, including Oktoberfest in Munich and La Merce in Barcelona. Oktoberfest is an 18-day mix of beer and carnival that originally celebrated a royal marriage.

The Mid-Autumn (Moon) Festival in China is an ancient celebration of the moon as a symbol of peaceful times and family reunion. Celebrated under September's full moon, families gather together to gaze up at the moon, light lanterns, make mooncakes and feast.

If you decide to spend an evening outside, why not light a fire and make Josie and Lisa's mac 'n' cheese (page 128), or get the whole family doing Laura's animal yoga in the moonlight (page 124)?

Kate, Spinney Hollow

Kate: The idea of what living sustainably means often overwhelms a lot of people ... or underwhelms them! While we live in woodland near Winchester, you absolutely don't have to go 'full hobbit' to live sustainably — it's just a matter of choice.

When you come to Camp Bestival, you will instantly recognise the world of Spinney Hollow, where every structure, tent and caravan is hand-stitched, dyed or whittled, and every activity on offer follows the same ethos. The joy on children's faces when they finish making their sword, wand, headdress, appliqué, macramé, jewellery or artwork makes it all worthwhile.

The response we get at Camp Bestival is amazing. We now have team of 70, all of us doing stuff with our hands and helping people engage in fun activities that don't cost the earth anything. Here are some thoughts about living a more sustainable life.

HOW TO LIVE SUSTAINABLY
*THROUGH THINKING, ACTING AND ENGAGING

THINK FIRST

The first thing is thinking. I'm not going to say 'buy this' or 'don't buy that', 'do this' or 'don't do that'. Instead, just think about what you buy. Do you need it? Is it single-use? Will it end up in a landfill? That said, we're big fans of Lego, which we argue is sustainable, as we reuse it over and over again. So just ask yourself, 'Is this environmentally positive?'. This can take time to research, and it can be hard and overwhelming, but it's worth doing.

I did listen to a programme once that said the most environmentally friendly thing you can do in your life (apart from going vegan or not having kids, ha ha!) is to check out where your pension's going. If everybody chose a good pension trust, it could change the world pretty quickly, because of what people's pensions are funding. Really think about where you are putting your money … there's a huge amount of money going into things you don't know about.

BE CONSCIOUS

Next up is being conscious, taking a bit of time so you can work out how to be part of the solution and not the problem. Then act on that. Actually do the stuff, don't just talk about it. There are people drinking out of their eco coffee cups and then not even batting an eyelid when they're off flying around the world or buying lots of plastic for Christmas. You have to be wary of that.

SHOP LOCALLY

Find out where you can buy locally grown food such as at local farm shops and that kind of thing. Maybe you could plant a little veg patch in a garden or even grow some herbs on a windowsill, just for the joy of thinking, 'Oh, I can do that!'. Another option is to use one of those veg box suppliers who sell veg that isn't perfect — because not everything is perfect.

ENGAGE

Now let's think about really engaging with stuff: getting involved with projects, interacting with things you're inspired by, chatting with people about what they're doing and why they're doing it. Community is such a big part of living a more sustainable life, because it helps you to share your thoughts and feelings, and find something to get involved in. Ask questions. Find out what your kids' school is doing, and whether they could do with help becoming more sustainable. Think about your office — is there anything they could be doing differently? Do they recycle the coffee pods, for example? Could they be doing more small things, and just caring more? It's about recognising we are only guardians of this lovely earth, and acknowledging that it does matter what we do. Being around positive people who don't think caring about these things is extreme really helps.

SMALL CHANGES CAN HAVE A BIG IMPACT

If you drink milk, drink organic or choose one recommended by the Soil Association. This means it's produced by smaller farmers. Rather than supporting industrialised farming, that monoculture, supporting smaller farmers is a bit more caring, a bit more thoughtful. And when you share that, other people will follow suit.

Look at what everyone around you is doing: get really engaged and show that you care. It's not just about what is happening in your house, it's about the community. People can get stuck; they might feel like everyone else is doing it, so they don't need to. This kind of attitude can have negative results. We all want a good future for our kids, so show them how to be the change.

Laura Lotus

Laura: My first contact with Robby was by post. It was the late 90s, and I was working in the music industry. I sent him promotional club vinyl. A few years later, I would see him and Josie at Triyoga, London, where we all attended yoga classes. It wasn't until I moved to the Isle of Wight a decade ago, though, that I really got to know and love them. I felt honoured to be invited to teach at Camp Bestival, and my role has since developed into gathering a team of yoga teachers to deliver a diverse yoga schedule up in the Slow Motion area.

Slow Motion buzzes with energy, with its packed yoga classes, sound baths, breath workshops, hot tubs, ice baths, sauna … it's a mini wellness festival in its own right. I love how eclectic the classes are. We get whole families coming along in their fancy dress; shattered parents desperate for an hour of 'me time' before getting stuck back in; performers and workers on their breaks

seeking to realign their bodies and minds (and sometimes needing an impromptu nap!). Last year, I had one teenage girl tell me she now felt the most relaxed she had since before Covid. Everyone is welcome. In Dorset, we enjoy the background sound of the peacocks calling, as well as music from the main stage, while in Shropshire, we look out over the lake, which is the most beautiful view I have ever had from a yoga mat.

Yoga means union, and at Camp Bestival, we unite yoga with music, family and nature. There is a magical atmosphere at this precious festival, where wonderful memories and lifelong friendships are made.

To enjoy some of this magic in your own home, clear a space and get ready to stretch. Try to hold each pose for 5—10 breaths. Yoga mats will make it more comfortable, but are not essential.

CAT STRETCH

Start on all fours and push down through your hands, lift your shoulders up to your ears, and tuck your chin in towards your heart.

LION'S BREATH

From cat stretch, breathe in, then push your tummy down towards the mat. Lift your head up and, as you breathe out, stick out your tongue as far as you can and make the sound of a lion with your breath: Haaaaah!

DOWNWARD DOG

Place your hands on the mat, shoulder width apart, and your feet hip distance apart. Lift your bottom up towards the ceiling. Look between your ankles to keep your back straight.

DOWNWARD DOG WITH A PARTNER (OR TWO!)

The first dog stays very still in downward dog position. The second one sets up in front of them, with their feet outside the first one's hands. Then, one foot at a time, they step up to place their feet on either side of the first person's tailbone. When it's time to come down, the second person steps down first.

COBRA

Lie on your tummy and place your hands on the mat, a bit wider than shoulder width apart. Press up with straight arms. For King Cobra, bend your legs, lean your head back, and see if you can scratch your head with your toes!

CAMEL

Kneel up (you might want to place a blanket under your knees) with your knees hip width apart and your toes tucked under. Start with your hands on hips and look forwards as you arch your back. If it feels good, you can reach back to catch hold of your ankles and slowly tip your head back. Be careful not to over stretch — listen to your body. You might want to go into a cat stretch after this to relax your back again.

DOUBLE BOAT

Facing your partner, bend your legs and hold hands. Place the soles of your feet to the soles of your partner's feet. Next, straighten one leg at a time, pointing your toes up towards the sky. Then lean back for a lovely back and leg stretch. If there are others with you, this makes a great tunnel for baby cobras to swim under!

LIZARD

From downward dog pose, lift one foot up high, then step it forward and place it on the mat outside your wrist. Keep your back leg straight, and your tummy low to the mat. Look forward if you can — and smile! Don't forget to swap over and do the other leg.

BIRD OF PARADISE

This is trickier than tree, but we love a challenge! Start in a forward bend with your feet wide, then tuck your right shoulder inside your right knee, while your left arm reaches behind you to clasp your other hand or hold on to your clothes. With your left leg firmly on the floor, come on to the tiptoes of your right foot. Look forward and press firmly through your left foot as you try and float your right leg up to the sky.

LIZARD ON A ROCK

This one is for two people. Partner number one is the rock. Come on to your knees and keep them together. Rest your forehead on the mat and put your arms back, tucking them in to the body. Partner number two is the sunbathing lizard, lying along the rock. Start by standing in front of the partner number one's feet, then very carefully lean on to their back until you are lying tailbone to tailbone, with your head resting against theirs. Stretch out your arms and legs when you are ready.

Tip: This is a great set of poses to use during Kukur Tihar, the Hindu festival that celebrates dogs and other animals in October and November.

Don't forget to lie down, stretch out and relax for a few minutes at the end.

family feast

EASY ONE-POT MACARONI CHEESE

Lisa: I met Josie at the school gates about 11 years ago. Our two eldest children were in the same class, and our two five-year-old boys had made friends. We arranged to meet up for a coffee for an hour or so, and six hours later, we were in love! Luckily, all six children and our husbands, Ben and Robby, love each other too and as a consequence we have spent many happy times together over the years.

We've been to Camp Bestival every year for the last ten years, so we've gone from watching Mr Tumble to raving in the Bollywood tent with our kids. It's so hard to pick out highlights from over the years, because there are so many, and often it's the little moments that really stay with you. I remember my son (then aged about seven) falling asleep in my arms (for the last time that I can recall) during Tears for Fears, or a really fantastic theatre group rolling along the upper kids' field, performing a space landing as they went by on a Sunday morning.

Our love of the outdoors unites our two families. Sailing, fishing, kayaking, paddleboarding, wild swimming, hiking, stargazing and, best of all, camping (and therefore, sitting around campfires). Cooking over a fire is a major part of that for me and Josie. We always come up with a plan beforehand, and we just really enjoy the process of cooking outdoors and producing something really

delicious and surprising. And once we've finished cooking, we just throw a few more logs on to the fire and have a beautiful evening of music, chatting and laughing. Fire, food, festoon lights, fun, family and friends — we really give an F!

You don't need anything special to cook on a campfire — just the fire. The point is to be able to do it anywhere. We've cooked surf and turf on a frozen beach on Christmas Eve! This macaroni cheese goes so nicely with a big pile of garlicky mushrooms and sausages, all super-easy campfire food. And don't forget the marshmallows for afters — shame to waste the embers!

1. Gently melt the butter in a saucepan over a low heat. Don't allow it to brown. Once the butter is melted, add the flour and cook gently for 2–3 minutes. Again, don't allow it to burn.

2. Add the water a little at a time, stirring constantly to avoid lumps. Bring the mixture to a simmer, then crumble in the stock cube and continue to stir until it's all nicely combined.

3. Add half the milk, stirring until fully combined, then add the rest. Continue to stir for around 5 minutes, until the mixture is simmering.

4. Add the mustard, if using, and mix well.

5. Add the dried pasta, and give it a really good stir to thoroughly coat the pasta and separate any clumps. Cover with a lid and cook for 10 minutes until the pasta has soaked up the liquid and is cooked through, stirring every few minutes and replacing the lid each time. The pasta will just stick to the bottom of the pan if you leave it. You can always add a drop more milk or water at this stage if you feel it's needed.

6. Remove the pan from the heat and add the cheese. Stir thoroughly until the cheese has melted, then cover with the lid and leave to stand for 5 minutes. This is now ready to eat, but if you're cooking other stuff on the fire, you can just put it to one side and reheat when you're ready— just loosen it up with a little extra milk or stock.

SERVES 4 (OR MORE IF YOU'RE HAVING IT AS A SIDE)

YOU WILL NEED:

2 heaped dessertspoons butter

3 heaped dessertspoons plain
flour

470ml water (hot or cold)

1 vegetable stock cube

470ml milk

2 heaped teaspoons Dijon or
English mustard (optional)

350g macaroni

250g ready-grated cheese – or
more, depending on how cheesy
you like it (we like a strong
Cheddar or a mix of whatever
is available – Cheddar, red
Leicester and Parmesan make a
fantastic combo)

Lisa Board

OCTOBER

did you know......

that the Anglo Saxons saw the end of October as marking

the beginning of winter?

get into nature

October is the most exciting time to watch deer. It's when rutting males compete for females to breed with. They bellow warnings to each other and, if that doesn't work, they walk beside each other before locking antlers in a battle of strength. The easiest way to see this is to visit some of our parklands. The best time to visit is three hours after dawn or at dusk. Keep your distance (and keep dogs on leads) at all times.

WHAT ELSE?

The last fruits are ripening, leaves are falling, and the days are getting colder and shorter. Swans and geese are starting to arrive for winter, and lots of our small animals are getting ready for the colder months. Have you seen the squirrels storing hazelnuts and acorns in the ground?

Garden birds need to fatten up this month, too, so why not reuse your Halloween pumpkins to make a bird feeder? Just scrape out as much flesh as possible, take off the top, make large holes in the sides and then push sticks around the outside for perches. Fill the pumpkin with bird seed and hang it somewhere that other animals can't reach.

Foraging

Rosehips and sloes (see page 116) are still around if you haven't picked some already.

Chestnuts and beech nuts fall from trees in parks, along roadsides and in woods at this time of year. The beech tree is easy to spot thanks to its dark purple leaves and wavy bark. Look for paired, three-sided nuts in bristly shells, and use them like pine nuts.

'Penny bun' mushrooms can be found growing in the grass around oak beech and birch trees. The tops look a bit like a miniature loaf, with white gills underneath and a very thick, brown stem. These are considered the most delicious of all wild mushrooms.

WEATHER

Now that we are past the equinox, days are getting shorter, and when the clocks go back at the end of the month, the evenings will get dark even earlier. But don't be disheartened by the short, damp days. There will still be some sunny days to enjoy, and there is plenty to forage and celebrate this month.

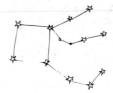

October's full moon is called the Hunter's Moon, because people used to hunt animals by moonlight at this time to stock up their winter store.

A good constellation to look for this month is Pegasus, which is just to the south-east of Cygnus. It looks like an empty square rather than a winged horse. This is because the stars that make the square body can be seen with the naked eye, but you'll need binoculars to see those that make up the wings and neck. It was the first constellation to be found outside of our solar system. According to Greek mythology, Pegasus sprang from the blood of Medusa's neck when Perseus cut off her snake-topped head.

Note: Always double-check you have correctly identified any mushrooms before you eat them.

Find inspiration in other CELEBRATIONS

A long time ago, our ancestors divided the year into the light half, starting with Beltane, and the dark half, after Samhain. The Celts believed in bringing in the harvest before Samhain so that it couldn't be damaged by the evil spirits that could enter our world on that day. Christians later called this festival All Hallows' Eve (the day before All Souls' Day), and would put out vegetables to keep the spirits happy. So you can see how we got Halloween and pumpkins.

In Mexico, they celebrate All Souls' Day as La Día de los Muertos (the Day of the Dead). On this day, they believe the veil between our world and the afterlife is at its thinnest and that they are briefly reunited with dead relatives to feast, drink and celebrate together.

This month, Eli da Bank shows us how to look like a skeleton before helping the family to make a feast fit for past souls — see pages 138 and 142.

Billy, Cirque Bijou & Claire, Extraordinary Bodies

When we want to make something extra special for Camp Bestival Billy is the man we call. Over the last few years, we have turned HMS *Bestival* into a pop-art show boat, lifted Gok Wan over the stage in a 10-metre heart, produced a show called Disco Inferno featuring the largest giant mirror ball in the world — and much more.

And when a spectacle requires dance, Claire Hodgson is the only person for the job — especially when we wanted to break the world record for the largest disco dance (which Claire led and taught). Together, Billy and Claire founded Extraordinary Bodies, a circus for everyone, featuring deaf, disabled and non-disabled artists. This is a magical space where diversity is welcome, boundaries are broken and inclusivity is key. When they are next in your town touring one of their incredible shows, don't miss it!!! In the meantime, you can have a go at creating your own Billy and Claire-style show …

HOW TO MAKE A SHOW TO PERFORM WITH YOUR FAMILY

STEP ONE: FIND INSPIRATION

This could be a piece of music, a picture, or a story you love. Talk about it with your family — they might suggest more songs or expand the story.

STEP TWO: WRITE THE STORY

This could be written down, painted or drawn as a series of pictures like a storyboard. Think first about introducing your characters and the world they live in. Is it in the future or a particular time in history? Next, find the drama, a problem they might be facing — like the imminent arrival of an alien spaceship. What are the aliens bringing? The ideas don't have to make everyday sense! Then, in the age-old traditions of the circus, celebrate the successful overcoming of the challenges in a big celebratory finale. Each character has their moment in the spotlight and shares their skills. We often think about having around five numbers or scenes.

STEP THREE: CHOOSE ROLES

Decide who is directing, who is choreographing, and who will be in the show. Everyone can join in with making props or choosing costumes. Share out the roles or perhaps swap around. You need a good outside eye to give feedback on scenes before you perform before an audience. This might mean different people taking on the role of director.

STEP FOUR: IDENTIFY YOUR SKILLS

Include everyone's skills, as well as your dogs, cats and any other pets! These are your 'circus' skills, which can be incorporated into your show. Can anyone balance objects, sing or play instruments? Does someone have flexible joints? Can anyone do a magic trick or disappearing act? Always remember to warm up and be safe.

STEP FIVE: REHEARSALS

This is the really fun part. Set out your stage, try out different ideas and then keep what works. Remember to listen to the quietest person in the room and treat all ideas with equal respect. Music is really important at this point, so choose a playlist that you can rehearse to. Think about a mixture of music. If you are all in the show, it might be useful to film your rehearsal so you can watch it back and make changes. Sleep on your ideas and give yourself breaks between rehearsals; this allows the best ideas to come up and make it through.

STEP SIX: INVITE AN AUDIENCE

Perform your show for friends, neighbours or family!

MAKE + CREATE

ELI's SKELETON FACE

Robby and Eli da Bank

YOU WILL NEED:

sponge

water

white face paint

black face paint

make-up brush or fine paintbrush

This is a super-simple face-painting idea for kids that even I (Dad) can just about get away with applying to a child's face without embarrassing them – or me! Seven-year-old Eli says: 'Skeletons are scary but I do like looking like one and scaring my granny or Mum. Sometimes it feels weird having a paintbrush on my face, but when I look in the mirror, it always looks really cool.'

1. Dampen the sponge with water and load it with some of the white face paint.

2. Sponge the white face paint over the face and lips, avoiding the eye area.

3. Draw a shape around the eyes with white paint using the brush. We went for quite square shapes with rounded edges. Fill in these shapes with black, using either the brush or the sponge.

4. Now create a shape on the nose with the white paint, then outline it with black using the brush. Fill it in with black, using either the brush or the sponge. Make sure you black out the septum.

5. Frame the face in black with the wide edge of the brush, then shade the cheekbones, chin and forehead as pictured.

6. With the narrowest part of the brush, draw two lines stretching from the corners of the mouth to the cheekbones, then add little vertical lines for the teeth.

7. Use the brush to paint in teeth between the vertical lines.

8. You can add a few crease lines on the forehead and around the nose for detail.

This looks great with any outfit, but is particularly effective with a skeleton costume or with a black hoodie! It's easy to make a skeleton outfit: just dress in old black clothes and use white household paint to draw bones on them. Just check with your parents first!

family feast

HALLOWEEN FEAST WITH THE DA BANK FAMILY

SERVES 4 – 6

SPOOKY GREEN SKULL

FOR THE HUMMUS

400g can of chickpeas

juice of ½ lemon

2 handfuls of fresh spinach

2 tablespoons freshly chopped coriander

2 garlic cloves

1 tablespoon olive oil

3 tablespoons tahini (if you have any)

pinch of paprika (if you have any)

pinch of salt

a good few grinds of black pepper

TO DECORATE

cucumbers, carrots, peppers, cherry tomatoes, almonds, olives, or any other vegetables you like

corn chips

1. Combine all the hummus ingredients in a blender. If you are using tahini, you may need a little less oil. Blend together to form a rough paste, adding a little more oil if necessary.

2. Tip the hummus on to a plate and spread it into a 'skull' shape, leaving space around it for decoration.

3. Use your chosen vegetables to make the face.

4. Arrange the corn chips around the skull to define its shape, then serve.

CHILLI-STUFFED PEPPER FACES

5–6 peppers

1 tablespoon olive oil, plus extra for brushing

1 onion, finely chopped

2–3 garlic cloves, finely chopped

2 celery sticks, finely sliced

1 teaspoon ground cumin

chilli flakes, to taste

750ml passata

280ml vegetable stock

400g can of red kidney beans, drained

400g can of butter beans, drained

400g can of cannellini beans, drained

400g can of black-eyed beans, drained

1 dessertspoon vinegar

2 teaspoons cacao powder (or a couple of squares of chocolate, grated)

salt and freshly ground pepper

1. Cut the tops off the peppers and set them aside to make hats. With a spoon scoop out the seeds and insides of the peppers.

2. Use a small, sharp knife to carve faces into the peppers. A series of triangular shapes is easiest (it's best for a grown-up to do this part!).

3. Brush the peppers with a little oil, then set aside.

4. Heat the oil in a large saucepan over a medium heat. Add the onion, garlic and celery, and cook gently for 5–10 minutes until the onion and celery are both soft.

5. Add the cumin and chilli flakes and stir, then add the passata and vegetable stock.

6. Once the mixture is bubbling, add the beans, vinegar and cacao, and season with salt and pepper. Leave to bubble gently for 30 minutes until the sauce has reduced to a nice, thick consistency.

7. Preheat the oven to 180°C/gas mark 4 and brush a baking tray with a little oil.

8. Scoop the hot bean chilli mixture into the raw peppers, then top them with the pepper 'hats'. Place on the prepared baking tray and bake for 40 minutes.

9. Serve and wait for screams!

We have four kids of different ages, from seven to 17, so it's tricky to get them all in the same room at the same time, let alone eating and cooking together! Somehow, though, our Halloween feasts always seem to work, as the teens find their inner children and the younger ones love it when the whole family cooks and eats together. Munching our way through the spooky green skull is everyone's favourite part!

Get your family and friends excited for Halloween with everyday foods made spooky and silly! This feast is perfect for sharing and scaring on chilly autumnal evenings.

The da Bank Family

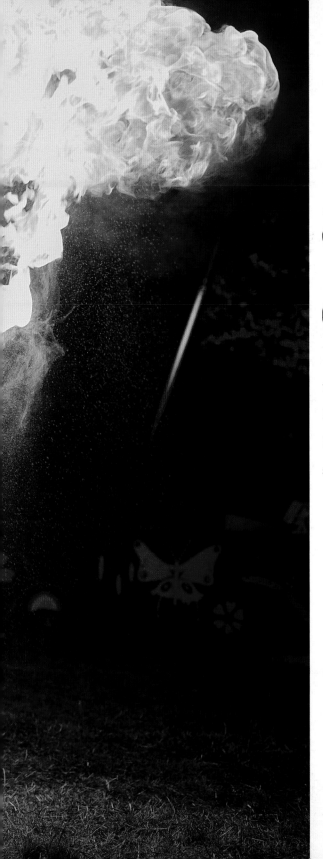

NOVEMBER

did you know.......

that the Saxons had an alternative name for the Roman's 'novem' (nineth) month? They called it Blot-Monath, or 'blood month', as they prepared stores of meat for the winter.

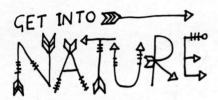

GET INTO NATURE

November may be a time when staying inside is really cosy, but the outside world still has some interesting surprises to offer. With the leaves gone, it is now possible to see birds' nests and squirrel dreys. It's also a great time to put on your wellies and kick up great piles of leaves as they lie on the ground in parks, woods and on roadsides.

Colder weather makes birds and animals flock together, and it is a good time to watch starlings and crows. These winter birds rely on late berries such as fat, rich ivy and holly for food. So don't forget to keep your bird table topped up this month. And look out for the strange fungi that November brings, such as cauliflower fungi and giant puffballs (see below)!

foraging

Puff balls look a bit like giant eggs, and can be found hiding under a hedge or in the corner of a field. Giant puff balls are about the size of a small football, and these are more delicious than their smaller cousins. If you are lucky enough to find one, try stuffing it with mince and herbs and baking it wrapped in bacon! Always double-check you have correctly identified any mushrooms before you eat them.

Holly and ivy can be used for decoration, so you might want to collect a few sprigs with berries. Store them in a vase of water, or weave them into a winter wreath using Spinney Hollow's headdress/wreath instructions on page 42. Ivy is poisonous and can irritate skin when handling. Please take care and always wash your hands after handling.

WEATHER

As the sun starts to move away from the northern hemisphere, the weather becomes colder and the nights start to draw in. In the north you might start to see the first overnight frosts of autumn.

November's full moon is known as the Frost Moon. This is a good month to spot the planets Mars, Jupiter and Saturn. Mars, which has a reddish colour, rises in the east, while Jupiter rises in the south-east and Saturn in the south. They are bigger and brighter than the stars around them, and do not twinkle.

We can also look for the constellation of Cetus to the south. Cetus (sometimes called 'the whale') was the sea monster sent to devour Princess Andromeda when her mother Cassiopeia boasted that she was more beautiful than the sea nymphs. Fortunately, the passing hero Perseus (of Medusa fame) killed the raging beast. The highlight of this constellation is the blue/orange double star marking the monster's mouth.

Find inspiration in other celebrations

The dark evenings are the perfect backdrop to fireworks and lantern lights. Diwali is a festival of lights and India's biggest and most important holiday of the year. There are different stories celebrated across India, but in each the light symbolises our inner light, which protects us from spiritual darkness.

In neighbouring Nepal, Tihar is celebrated at the same time. It takes place over five days, with each day dedicated to a different animal with a spiritual meaning. On day one, crows are honoured as messengers of the god of death. On day two, dogs are celebrated for their loyalty. Cows are honoured on day three, and oxen on day four, while the last day celebrates siblings. To celebrate, people put flower garlands around animal's necks and give them treats! If you don't have a dog, you can treat someone else's — or why not celebrate with Lisa's yoga downward dog (page 000)? And don't forget to make Kathy's fabulous lantern to celebrate Diwali.

Chris Tofu, Continental Drifts
(Caravanserai music maestro)

Chris Tofu is in our top three favourite menfolk. He
might even be number one. From being in the folk-
punk band the Tofu Love Frogs to curating many of the
coolest left-field stages at Glastonbury, smashing every
dance floor he plays with his mental mix of mash-ups,
and programming our beloved Caravanserai venue at
Camp Bestival, Chris is a force to be reckoned with.

 # CREATE THE PERFECT PARTY PLAYLIST

Chris: Festivals are all about the shared experience. Sometimes, the further the DJ is from the audience, the worse the vibe.

It's worth bearing in mind that DJing isn't rocket science. It's about reading the crowd and knowing what will make them have the best time possible, as well as trusting your choices and sometimes being a total clown. I love finding those songs that we all know, but done differently, whether that's a drum-and-bass recreation of a nursery rhyme or a crazy version of a Daft Punk song. People will revel in the recognition and even sing along.

In the 21st century, the DJ's 'record box' has expanded to millions of boxes, and it's quite daunting finding those bangers — there's almost too much choice. Sick versions sing out to you. You're looking for audience nirvana, which might come in the form of the whole audience singing along, collective arm-raising, or that strange sound not unlike a crowd on a roller coaster when the bass hits, especially if it does so in a surprising way.

If you find a mash-up, remix or plain bonkers version of a song you love, a really helpful tip is to then look for the artist responsible on Spotify or Deezer, and search through their playlist.

Don't conform to the one style; try finding songs that will move the audience in different ways while still holding their attention. For instance, you can easily mix drum and bass and rock 'n' roll as they have similar BPMs, but they sound completely different.

Finally, remember to play those tunes with joy, and respect that someone else is listening to what you're doing; some DJs treat the whole festival thing like they're sending emails or relentlessly packing eggs on a production line. For the best vibes, LOVE what you're playing — as you should — and the audience will surely see that and follow along.

Here are some of my favourite tunes to include on a playlist:

TJR — 'Funky Vodka (Original Mix)'

WBBL — 'Whole Lotta Wob'

Phil Mac & The Bellinis — 'Song 2'

Basement Jaxx — 'Bingo Bango'

Ed Solo & Deekline — 'King Of The Bongo'

Lily Allen — 'Smile (Mista Trick & Fizzy Gillespie Remix)'

AC/DC — 'Highway to Hell'

Toots and the Maytals — '54-46 (That's My Number)'

Nia Archives — 'Baianá'

Jackson 5 — 'I Want You Back (Billy Hole Samba Remix)'

MAKE & CREATE

DIWALI LANTERN

YOU WILL NEED:

plastic bottle
scissors
coloured paper
glue stick
tissue paper

sticky tape
LED tealight
piece of bamboo or
   stick (optional)

Kathy, CB Creative Crew

Kathy: I'm officially a Bestival Old Girl, having worked at every Bestival and then Camp Bestival from the very start, so I'm pretty much part of the furniture (a camping chair, maybe).

I started out at Bestival in 2004 doing the sign-writing, kneeling on the grass around the back of the Bollywood tent covered in gloss paint. Now I run the Camp Bestival Creative Studio, producing millions of miles of bunting and a multitude of textiles, flags, artwork, installations, signs, archways, sets, stages and more.

The creative team is really at the heart of each show, with tons of planning going into making every year look and feel better than ever. I love my job and feel very fortunate to be part of the Camp Bestival family. I still feel a huge buzz of excitement going onsite each year. It's a place where I've had some of my most brilliant experiences, learned so much and made lifelong friends.

Our Bollywood tent is a Camp Bestival staple and a firm favourite. Hanging from the ceiling inside it are all sorts of lanterns — and here's one you can make at home. They are perfect for this month's celebration of light. Take inspiration from our lantern parade and see what you can come up with.

1. Carefully cut the plastic bottle in half, you'll just need the bottom half.

2. Cut a strip of coloured paper that is just long enough to wrap around the bottle and overlap by about a finger's width, and wide enough to cover the bottom half of the bottle.

3. Take some more coloured paper and cut it to the same size as the first piece, then cut this strip into equal-sized squares.

4. Roll up each square diagonally and glue the ends together, then glue each roll to the long strip until the strip is almost covered in rolls (leave a bit at the end).

5. Decorate the rolls by adding some flower shapes. If you like, you can design and cut out your own, but I've used a stamp here. Glue the flower shapes to the centre of each roll.

6. Take a piece of tissue paper the same length as the main strip of paper and slice into it to create a fringe, leaving the top part intact.

7. Tape the top of the tissue paper to the bottom of the bottle.

8. Cut a thin strip of coloured paper and tape it across the top of the bottle to make a handle.

9. Take the strip of paper decorated with the rolls and wrap it around the bottle, then glue it in place where it overlaps.

10. Drop in your LED tea light and you have a lantern!

11. If you have a long stick or piece of bamboo, you can attach the lantern to the top.

family feast
COOKING ON A BUDGET

Ben & Holly

BEN'S JERK CHICKEN WRAPS WITH RICE AND PEAS

SERVES 6

YOU WILL NEED:

10 pieces of chicken thighs, bone in (or joint 1 whole chicken)

2 tablespoons jerk chicken paste (or 1 tablespoon jerk seasoning powder mixed with 2 tablespoons natural yogurt)

FOR THE RICE AND PEAS

400g can of red kidney beans or black-eyed beans, rinsed and drained

400ml can of coconut milk

2–3 thyme sprigs

¼ teaspoon allspice

100ml water

1 Scotch bonnet chilli, left whole

450g long-grain rice, washed

25g butter

3 spring onions, chopped, or 1 small onion, finely chopped, plus extra to serve

3 garlic cloves, finely chopped

salt and freshly ground black pepper

TO SERVE

6 tortilla wraps

natural yogurt

freshly chopped coriander

Ben and Holly have worked with our team for the last ten years, creating the Grazing Garden at Bestival and the Brunch Club at Camp Bestival — and most recently producing and curating the Feast Collective.

Their jerk chicken wraps served with rice and peas are great to cook at any time of the year, and a great option if you're catering for a large gang. We fired up the barbecue and fed these to the creative team at this year's Camp Bestival.

1. Rub the chicken with the jerk paste, then cover and leave in the fridge overnight to marinate.

2. The next day, preheat a barbecue and cook the chicken slowly for 40 minutes, turning frequently until cooked through. You may find it easier to cook the chicken in the oven at 180°C/gas mark 4 for 30 minutes, and then transfer it to the barbecue for the last 15 minutes to get that smoky flavour.

3. Meanwhile, to make the rice and peas, combine the beans, coconut milk, thyme, allspice, water, chilli and salt and pepper in a saucepan over a low heat and bring to a gentle simmer. Add the rice.

4. In a separate pan, melt the butter over a low heat. Add the onion and garlic and fry for 5 minutes.

5. When the rice has been cooking for 10 minutes, add the garlic and onion to the pan, then cover with a lid and cook for a further 5 minutes over a low heat. Make sure the rice doesn't stick to the bottom of the pan.

6. To serve, take a wrap and spoon some rice and peas into the middle. Shred the chicken with two forks and pile some on top of the rice, then add a dollop of yogurt. Garnish with fresh coriander and more spring onions, then tuck in the ends and roll.

This is a really easy thing to make for a summer barbecue and doesn't require any cutlery or crockery — which means less washing-up!

Tip: For a vegetarian option, use jackfruit instead of chicken and pan-fry for around 10 minutes.

Winter might be seen as a dark, boring season, but if we didn't get that downtime after a busy year, I think we'd all miss it. The Isle of Wight really does shut down, with very few tourists and not much happening. We love the challenge of filling longer evenings with the kids and having more family time … but we wouldn't want it to be any longer!

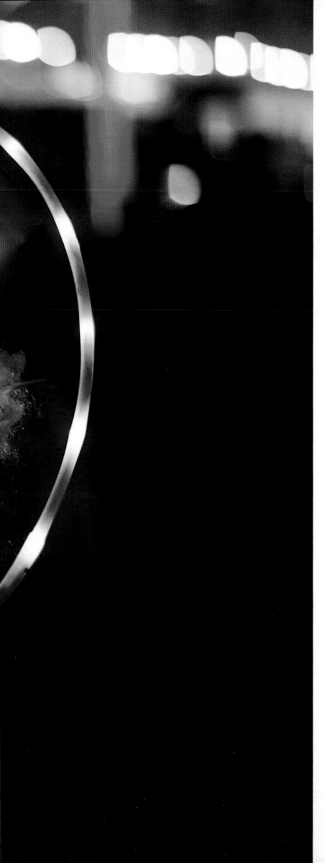

DECEMBER
did you know......

that December originally only had 30 days in the month? This was according to the old Roman calendar, but when the Julian calendar was adopted in the 1st century BCE, December gained another day.

GET INTO NATURE

Are you enjoying the winter landscape? Bare trees and low sunsets can look quite magical. Some of our small animals are in hibernation now, but December is the one of the best times for bird-watching from your window as our feathered friends visit easy feeding grounds. If you have a bird feeder, you might see some Scandinavian visitors, like blackcaps, fieldfares, redwings and waxwings. Winter birds need high-fat food to help them keep warm, such as suet and peanuts. Why not look up what different birds look like and keep your binoculars near the window?

WHAT ELSE?

With less food in the wild, foxes and badgers come closer to houses, looking for food in bins and gardens. Slugs are hibernating in the soil, while snails seal themselves into their shells with a thick layer of slime. London plane trees look like Christmas trees at this time, with furry seed baubles dangling from their branches. Identifying other trees becomes much harder as most have lost their leaves. See if you can see identify five different tree types.

FORAGING

Winter branches can be gathered at this time to make a wreath. If you haven't picked some holly yet, get some now to tuck into your Christmas wreath, and use any leftover bits to make a table decoration. You might even find mistletoe growing on trees in parks.

Fungi can still be picked now. Look around rotten wood and at the base of trees for chanterelles, honey fungus and fairy-ring mushrooms. Always double-check you have correctly identified any mushrooms before you eat them.

Pine needles can be gathered and brewed into pine needle tea for a natural cold remedy.

WEATHER

Did you know that the words for 'wet' and 'water' come from the same word as 'winter'?

The Winter Solstice occurs around 21 December, when the Earth's tilt away from the sun is at its maximum. The sun is at its lowest point in the sky, so we see the shortest daylight hours. The darkest week of the year is the week before the Solstice.

December's full moon is the Oak Moon. This may be because the oak is strong and stable, important characteristics when it comes to surviving winter.

Mars is at its closest point to Earth this month. It can be found in the east. Remember, planets do not twinkle (only stars do), so look for a steady, reddish light. Once you've spotted it, search for the constellation of Taurus next to it. Taurus (the bull) is one of the most magnificent and interesting constellations in the sky. In Greek mythology, the god Zeus turned himself into a bull to carry Princess Europa off to the island of Crete. Marking the glinting eye of the bull is Aldebaran, its brightest (twinkling) star.

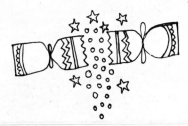

Find inspiration in other Celebrations

Decorating our houses with evergreens is an old tradition dating back to pagan Winter Solstice celebrations. The burning of the Yule Log is another winter tradition that many people in the UK still enjoy as part of their modern Christmas celebrations.

Romans held the feast of Saturnalia to honour Saturn, their god of farming, and to give thanks to the light after the Winter Solstice. This was a day when all the rules were reversed, with men dressing as women, servants becoming masters, and teachers becoming pupils!

Josie da Bank

Robby: Every year, Josie says to me that we're going to have a 'nice, simple Christmas', but luckily she's a secret sucker for all things festive and by 1 December, the house looks like Winter Wonderland on steroids. This suits me, as I love Christmas too. When Josie says her mantra is 'more is more', she's not lying. Walking into our kitchen is like being in Santa's Grotto itself.

This is the one time of the year when I actually sit down on a sofa and relax … well, for about 10 minutes, until the next lot of animals need feeding or dirty dishes need doing. What I really like about our Christmases is that most of the decorations are handmade, and it gives the house a really authentic feel. It doesn't need to be expensive bits bought from a shop.

DECORATE YOUR HOME AT CHRISTMAS

Josie: If you have been to Camp Bestival, you will know that my mantra is 'more is more' when it comes to decorating. More colour, more texture, more fun! Most importantly, though, I reuse decorations year after year.

I feel like the more effort that goes into the detail, the more special the event feels and the better it turns out. So I like to bring this feeling home and set the scene for the festive period.

I've been decorating my kitchen with these 'honeycomb' decorations for over 10 years. I like to mix them up with homemade decorations like my space rockets or the lovely decs the kids made at infant and junior school that I will never throw away. Some years are more elaborate than others, with tinsel, pompoms and paperchains mixed in, reminding me of a very tacky panto! Other years, I choose a colour palette and tone it down — a little!

A really fab thing about this way of decorating is that it takes very little time, yet friends think it's taken ages.

One of my secret weapons is using removable wall hooks! These are super-strong, sticky little hooks that leave no trace on your walls and don't require any power-tool skills, nails or fixings. You can find them online and in hardware shops, and you can achieve quite a lot around the house with these little things. Other useful items include cotton, thread, ribbon, paper clips, scissors, festive music and a chair or ladders (unless you have a tall husband). Plus a vague plan in your head of what you want to achieve.

I usually go for it on 1 December while the kids are at school, so it's a nice surprise when they get home. Start by sticking up all the hooks — and do follow the instructions on the packet, as you need to wait a while after sticking them up before you can use them for hanging. I like to put them above our kitchen island, and then I go for it, hanging colour over colour and layering it all up.

When the kids arrive home, I enjoy seeing their smiley little faces. Even super-cool 17-year-old Arlo can't help but smile and give me a hug.

CHRISTMAS BAUBLES

Cara Kane

YOU WILL NEED:

old Christmas bauble(s) in need of a revamp

string

ruler

wrapping paper offcuts

pencil

scissors or scalpel and mat (you may need an adult to help if using a scalpel)

glue (I like Mod Podge, but PVA is perfectly good)

small brush for the glue

ribbon

Clara: I started working for Camp Bestival during its inception year, 2008. Having spent some of my own childhood at music festivals, I shared Josie and Robby's passion for creating a festival environment for children and families. No one was doing a family festival back then. Robby and Josie's oldest son, Arlo, was two years old, and their second, Merlin, had just been born. Following a stint of work experience at Sunday Best (Robby's record label), I was brought on as Robby's assistant to help him juggle his extremely busy life. Arlo is now 17 and things have only got busier.

Last year I had my own daughter, Olive, who is not yet two and has already attended four Camp Bestivals (OK, she was in my tummy for one of them). It's no wonder that she absolutely loves it!

My professional role has morphed into a completely different set of responsibilities these days. As senior creative producer, I work closely with Josie to realise her ever-evolving ideas for the festivals. We have created unique stages and staged many spectaculars throughout the years, as well as building multiple bars, venues and shows. Josie has a creative mind, with an imagination that still surprises me on a weekly basis and a brilliant business head that she is far too modest to ever mention. It's an honour to be a part of this extraordinary team. Thank you, Camp Bestival, for the endless possibilities and unwavering support.

I made Josie some upcycled baubles as a gift last Christmas. She really loved them, and wanted me to share them with you.

1. Remove the top piece of the bauble, if it comes off. I have found that most do. This step is not vital, it just looks neater at the end if you can remove and then replace the top after the transformation is complete.

2. Use a piece of string to determine the circumference of the bauble around its widest part. Measure this length, then add 2cm (so if the circumference measures 10cm, your new measurement will be 12cm).

3. On the back of an old piece of wrapping paper (not too thick, because it can get tricky) draw a rectangle — the long edge should measure the circumference of the bauble, plus 2cm, while the short edge should measure just the circumference of the bauble.

4. With a pencil, make a mark every 5mm along the short edge, then cut the wrapping paper into 5mm wide strips. You can use either scissors or a scalpel, ruler and mat, whichever you are most comfortable with.

5. Starting at the top (neck) of the bauble, use a small brush to paint your first line of glue around the bauble. Place the first strip of paper on to the glue, ensuring it is perfectly straight. Repeat this step until the whole ball is covered.

6. Replace the top piece of the bauble if you removed it at the start, and add some ribbon to finish it off.

family feast

TURKEY ON THE GRILL

SERVES 6

YOU WILL NEED:

FOR THE TURKEY

6kg slow-grown organic
　turkey from your local
　butcher (or there are
　some great online
　butchers)
extra virgin olive oil,
　for drizzling
4 tablespoons freshly
　chopped sage

FOR THE BRINE

1 litre hot water
200g fine salt
4 onions, halved
2 garlic bulbs, halved
6 bay leaves
big bunch of sage
big bunch of thyme
big bunch of rosemary
250g soft dark brown sugar
4 tablespoons toasted
　coriander seeds
2 tablespoons black
　peppercorns
3 litres cold water

FOR THE GRAVY

2 tablespoons plain flour
2 tablespoons wholegrain
　mustard
200ml white wine
1 litre chicken stock

YOU WILL ALSO NEED:

a large pot and fridge, or
　a cool box and 2 frozen
　freezer blocks (for the
　brining)
a lidded grill/barbecue that
　is set to 150°C

When it comes to all things carnivorous — steaks, the tastiest burgers, ribs and occasionally a bit of blood — our friends DJ BBQ and Chris 'Chops' Taylor are right up there with barbecue royalty.

Chops and DJ BBQ: Why use up space in your kitchen oven when you can cook outdoors and create a centrepiece that not only tastes good but brings the family together with friends and hungry dogs alike? All you need is a simple barbecue with a lid and some wood or charcoal.

We like to use slow-grown organic turkeys for Christmas, but the most important thing is to buy the best you can afford. A slow-grown bird will have a higher fat content and will give you a juicier roasted turkey. If you have time, brine your turkey; this will impart seasoning and flavour, and, most importantly, will help keep those all-important juices flowing. It's best to brine your turkey two days before, but overnight will be fine.

Make sure you use some decent British charcoal and wood to cook with, as you want there to be no chemicals and a light smoke. And it's very important to use as many fresh herbs as you can in the brine. You can always lay them on the turkey when you roast it, too. Have a go at our recipe below.

1.　In a large pot, combine all the brine ingredients except the cold water. Place over a medium heat and warm through until the sugar has dissolved, then take off the heat and stir in the cold water.

2.　If the pot is large enough to fit the whole turkey (and you have room for it in your fridge), you can use the pot. If not, prepare a large cool box that is big enough to fit the whole turkey.

3.　Remove the giblets from the turkey and add them to the brine mix. Add the turkey to the pot and place in the fridge, or place the turkey into the cool box and pour over the brine to cover. Add a freezer block and seal, then leave in a cool place. Use a probe to check the temperature stays below 5°C, and replace the freezer block as needed to keep the temperature down.

4.　Set up and preheat your barbecue to 150°C. Make two small coal beds on either side of the grill.

5.　Remove your turkey from the brine and leave it to drain. Strain the brine. Start the gravy by tipping the strained brine veg and giblets into a roasting tray and roasting for 30 minutes on the grill. Remove the roasted veg, then add the flour, mustard, white wine and chicken stock to the tray. Bring to the boil for about 20 minutes, then strain through a sieve and set aside.

6. Now time for that glorious bird. Lightly drizzle the turkey with some extra virgin olive oil and season with salt, pepper and the chopped sage. Place the turkey on the grill — bam! Straight in the middle of the grill. Cook it breast-side up for 30 minutes, then turn over so it's breast-side down and leave it for another 20 minutes. Turn it back over and roast breast-side up until the internal temperature reaches 68°C.

7. Rest the turkey in a warm place for at least an hour before you carve. As you rest the turkey, the internal temperature will keep increasing, getting past that all-important 72°C.

8. It's carving time. This is where so many people make a silly decision and just carve slices off the breasts. This is as ridiculous as thinking that Mick Hucknall's voice is anything other than lovely (and don't get me started on how great the rhythm section is). In our humble opinion, the best way is to remove the whole breast and then slice that juicy goodness. For the rest of the bird, tear off pieces of that smoky turkey like some sort of labrador. Keep the oysters for yourself — bam. Enjoy!

Chops & DJ BBQ

HAPPY NEW YEAR

JANUARY

did you know........

that the month of January takes its name from Janus,

the Roman god of new beginnings and change?

Get into Nature

Kick off the New Year with long winter walks and you are likely to see squirrels and robins.

If you visit a beach, you may see some mysterious, jelly-like ocean drifters. Jellyfish get washed up in large numbers this month, as do smaller creatures called 'by-the-wind sailors'. These have bluish jelly bodies and a sail-shaped top that catches the wind. Watch out for the poisonous Portuguese man o' war jellyfish, which is much larger and has a large 'float' that looks like an old, pinkish-purple balloon. Be careful — they can still sting.

WHAT ELSE?

Cold days with either frost or snow are a good time to try identifying footprints. Bird prints are always fun to look at, and it's surprising how many different prints you spot. Why don't you photograph any that you don't recognise, and then look them up when you get home? Look out for the first signs of snowdrops, crocuses and daffodils as you wander. And why not plant up some pots with spring bulbs, such as hyacinths and dwarf daffodils, which you can grow inside?

FORAGING

At this time of year, nature is very still — sleeping, perhaps? Even the animals are struggling to forage, and hunger is making them braver and forcing them to travel further to find food.

There are still many fungi in the woods (always double-check you have correctly identified any mushrooms before you eat them). And have you collected any rosehips or pine needles? If not, now is your last chance to pick them to make natural cold remedies.

WEATHER

January may be the coldest month, but now that we are past the Winter Solstice, the days are getting longer. The low position of the sun at this time of year makes for beautiful wintery sunsets.

January's full moon is called the Wolf Moon because in countries where wolves live, they are active at this time of year and often howl at the moon on cold nights.

Did you know that the constellation Orion lies close to the equator and so can be seen by everyone at the same time? We see Orion in the south-west of our sky. Orion's Belt contains some of our brightest and best-known stars: Alnitak, Alnilam and Mintaka. If you trace the belt from left to right, it points to the planet Mars.

According to Greek mythology, the formidable hunter Orion was the most handsome man on earth. He used his ability to walk on water to enter the Greek island of Chios, where he got into trouble and was killed by a scorpion. Zeus threw Orion and the scorpion into opposite sides of the sky.

Find Inspiration in Other Celebrations

As we've seen, the Roman calendar used to be made up of just ten months, with a gap between December and March. Eventually, one of the Roman emperors was forced to recognise the period after December, and January and February were named.

Today's New Year celebrations borrow much from traditional Scottish festivals such as Hogmanay and Up Helly Aa, which involved a symbolic burning of the old to make way for the new, and traditions in ancient China, where fireworks were lit to scare off the devil and welcome in prosperity and good luck.

Other 'modern' traditions around the globe include: going to the beach in Brazil and jumping seven waves while making seven wishes; eating 12 grapes (one for each strike of the clock) in Spain; and watching the ball drop in New York's Times Square. In Denmark, they throw old plates at their friends' doors to wish them luck (tradition says the more broken kitchenware on your doorstep, the better off you'll be). The Canadians go ice-fishing, while the Greeks hang onions on their doors!

Whatever you do, we wish you a year filled with awesome nature, laughter, family and making fun things together.

Kwame Bakoji-Hume (African Activities)

HOW TO INSPIRE YOUR KIDS TO LOVE MUSIC

Kwame: My grandfather was a musician and my father was a drummer. They didn't ask us to learn music, but we got into it anyway. When we heard the rhythms in the house, we made our own drums and started making music from pans and other things we found: cooking utensils, stirring sticks — whatever was lying about. We'd be cooking with our mums and instead of stirring the rice, we'd be tapping the pot, creating our own music.

I do think it can make children more interested in music if there's a musician, or at least some music, in the house. Kids love the simplicity, the rhythm, and how catchy music is, so just teach them to sing simple songs. Make it as easy as possible — for you and them. No pressure.

If you have no musicians in your family, or are very shy, what you need to do is get your children to see music out and about. Take them to a workshop, a community thing, or a festival like Camp Bestival if you can!

You don't have to have a musical instrument at home to encourage your kids to make their own music. If you're sitting down in the lounge, just start tapping a rhythm on the sofa arms! Or take two books and just clap them together to make different sounds. Pick any old rubbish from your house, and you'll discover anything can be a musical instrument!

Kids want to make music. It's interesting to them. They see it on TV and hear it on the radio, and they wanna play it. Kids' minds open when they see a drum and hear it played for the first time. It's so simple. They ask me, 'Are you really a drummer? Can I touch the drum?!' When they see a real instrument, they are fascinated by the idea that music can come from it.

Make it simple — that's what music is about. TVs and screens distract kids from reality. It's not bad having devices in your house, but what they see inside the screens should be things they also do in reality. If they see forests and beaches on TV, try and get them to see those things in real life. If they see bands and DJs and musicians on screen, get them to experience them in real life if you get the chance. Seeing music live, like at a festival, means it's real. They can touch it... they can feel it!

Music is a beautiful thing to share, and having a go at making it will give your kids the confidence to explore it further.

MAKE +CREATE A LOO ROLL
with Josie

Josie da Bank

YOU WILL NEED:

cardboard
scissors
double-sided sticky tape
toilet roll inner tube
masking tape
pipe cleaners

wrapping paper
tissue paper
glue
paints (acrylic or poster)
paintbrush

Around 20 years ago, I bought my favourite Christmas decorations ever from the Conran shop. Now, every year, I can't wait to get them out and hang them in the kitchen. What are they? Space rockets! OK, the Conran shop versions aren't made from loo rolls, but I do think these homemade rockets are just as special. Over the years, I've had a go at making different versions with all four boys. One year, I went all out and made a larger version for the 'elf on a shelf' to fly in on 1 December. This is a great way to use up any wrapping paper offcuts.

Enjoy!

1. On your piece of cardboard, draw two wings the same length as your toilet roll tube, along with a tail. Then draw a circle with a 7cm diameter.

2. Cut out the four pattern pieces. Take the circle and snip out a quarter of it as shown.

3. Fold along the edge of the tail and wing pieces, as shown.

4. To make the nose cone, attach the two cut sides of the circle together using double-sided tape.

5. Attach the tail and wings to the tube using double-sided sticky tape, then use masking tape to attach the cone to head of the tube.

6. Make a small hole in the centre of the tube at the top and insert a pipe cleaner to use as a handle. Twist together the ends inside the tube to secure.

7. Using your wrapping paper offcuts and tissue paper, decorate the rocket, using glue to fix them in place. You can use paint to add stripes or other details. If you don't have wrapping paper, try using tissue, sweet wrappers, glitter or foil — whatever you have to hand!

8. If you like, you can insert more pipe cleaners into the back end of the tube and secure them in place with a bit of tape, then curl them to look like flames.

9. Zooooom around the room making rocket noises!

family feast

THREE-CHEESE CAULIFLOWER

Fatboy Slim: This is, without doubt, my greatest hit as a cook. Grown-ups always request it with any roast I make, while my younger diners swear it is the only thing I cook that is to their taste. It has even got me props from in-laws. The key is to include three different cheeses and generous amounts of mustard. The tang is the thang! Make generous portions, because it is even tastier reheated the next day.

For the three cheeses, Gruyère is a 'must', and is good mixed with mature Cheddar. On top of that, add whatever you have lying around in the fridge as the 'guest' cheese; it could be Parmesan, anything blue, or just that random flavoured cheese that you've had lying around for ages and never knew what to do with. The cocktail of three different cheeses is the key to the depth of flavour of this dish.

You can also add other elements. Parboiled broccoli goes fabulously or you could add chopped bacon for a salty hit or raw onion for extra tang. Tinned sweetcorn sweetens it up for the younger ones.

1. Preheat the oven to 180°C/gas mark 4.

2. Pour the milk into a saucepan. Add the onion and bay leaves and place over a medium heat. Bring to a simmer, then immediately take off the heat and leave to stew for at least 20 minutes, longer if possible. You have to watch the milk like a hawk while heating, as it goes from nothing to boiling over in about 3 seconds!

3. Break the cauliflower into large florets and parboil in a pan of salted water for 4 minutes. Drain immediately and tip into an ovenproof dish, spreading out the florets into an even layer.

4. Melt the butter in a small saucepan over a low heat. Add the flour and mix to make a roux. Cook for a few minutes (do this for a bit longer than you think; it should start to smell really nutty!).

5. Remove the onion and bay leaf from the milk and skim off any skin that's formed on top. Add the milk to the roux gradually, stirring continuously, until it turns into a thick but still essentially liquid sauce. If it feels a bit too gluey, then add more cold milk. Cook for a further couple of minutes to make sure the flour is all cooked.

6. Stir in the mustard powder; you should get a nice yellow hue.

7. Gradually stir in three-quarters of the cheese, making sure it doesn't separate.

8. Pour the cheesy sauce evenly over the top of the cauliflower. Do not stir; just pour it on top, trying to cover all the florets. As it cooks, it will diffuse through the cauliflower without going sloppy…

9. Sprinkle the rest of the cheese and breadcrumbs over the top, then bake in the oven for 25 minutes. This should give you a beautiful, browned and crunchy topping. Slide it on to the table and serve.

Enjoy.

Fatboy Slim

YOU WILL NEED:

400ml whole milk

½ onion

2 bay leaves

1 large cauliflower

50g butter

40g plain flour

2 teaspoons English mustard powder

150g three different cheeses in total – one MUST be Gruyère

2 tablespoons breadcrumbs (preferably panko)

FEBRUARY

did you know......

that to make the year add up to 365 days, February (which was named after the Roman god Februus) was only given 28 days? Romans honoured their dead during this period, meaning it was already considered an unlucky month… so they thought, why not keep it short?

≫ get into nature ≪

Nature is waking up after its winter sleep and signs of new life are out there, waiting to be discovered. Most of the year's first flowers are white. Snowdrops and wood anemones are in full flower at this time, and the first signs of leaves can be seen on the trees. Catkins dangle from branches and bumble bees start to come out of their winter hidey-holes. Small animals and birds are becoming more active and are about to start spring's courting.

In water, frogs and toads are some of the first to spawn. A female of these species can lay up to 3,000 eggs — which is just as well, because so many other animals like to eat them! Frogs and toads are most likely to spawn during sunny spells in still, shallow water.

WHAT ELSE?

Now is a good time to spot animals in the woods, because the longer days and bare trees make it easier to see what's happening. Larger animals such as badgers and foxes have been carrying young all winter and are now getting ready to give birth.

Foraging

We have been looking for leftover fruit and nuts for months, but now the first shoots, leaves and early flowers bring fresh life to our tables.

Early nettle tips and chickweed leaves are vitamin-rich, and nice and tender.

Early wild garlic can be found along the sunny side of hedges and damp woodland.

Violets and dandelion flowers should start to appear by the end of the month; these are good for making winter salads or baking that bit more special.

WEATHER

We have passed through January, the coldest month, but have we had snow? If not, it could still happen this month. We need very cold air to blow in from places like Siberia and the Arctic. This is why the north of Britain has more snow than the south — the north is closer to these regions of very cold air.

February's full moon is called the Snow Moon because this is the snowiest month for most countries north of the equator.

Last month, we looked for Orion the hunter in the south-west of our night sky. Now, let's look for Canis Major (the Great Dog), the larger of Orion's two hunting dogs. This constellation contains Sirius, the Dog Star, the brightest star in the sky. The Great Dog may be chasing Lepus, the Hare, a faint constellation visible below Orion. But another story is that Sirius was placed in the heavens after being caught up in an endless chase with an unbeatable fox.

snow moon

FiND inspiration from Other Celebrations ☆

Traditional February festivals would have involved the burning of fires to bring renewed life. The pagan festival Imbolc (which means 'in milk') was a celebration of the sheep and cows starting to produce milk again. Eggs are another sign that spring is on its way. In Maharashtra, India, they celebrate the hatching of turtles with the Velas Turtle Festival.

We need both eggs and milk for pancake-making on Shrove Tuesday. Did you know that pancake races started in 1445? A housewife was cooking pancakes when the church bells started to chime, and, not wanting to be late, she ran to the church with the frying pan still in her hand!

The end of winter is also a time for falling in love. Saint Valentine's Day was a celebrated feast day on which it was customary to choose a sweetheart. This Valentine's Day, show someone you love them by making them something. Why not try making Kathy's Camp Bestival Love-Bot on page 202, or Dave's secret recipe for chocolate-dipped flapjack on page 204? Delicious!

Sophie Ellis-Bextor

We asked everyone's favourite lady of kitchen discos to share her secret formula for lifting your family's spirits when it's all going a bit Pete Tong. If Sophie can't inject some pizazz and positive energy into your family parties, then no one can!

# HAVE THE BEST KITCHEN DISCO

Sophie: The kitchen disco that people associate me with was born out of a time when we couldn't go anywhere. We couldn't even go to other people's houses, let alone the gigs or festivals that had been such a big part of our lives!

So, at the start of the UK's national lockdown in 2020, we found ourselves and our five sons (ranging in ages from 14 months to 15 years) wondering what else we could do.

I felt very cut off, discombobulated, quite depressed and quite anxious (like lots of people). The news was very heavy-going. I was feeling a bit useless, and I missed people. But looking at social media, there were people doing all sorts of lovely things to help others feel connected. What could I do?

Richard (my husband) suggested, 'Why don't we livestream you singing and doing a live party set from home?'

And I thought, 'That's a bonkers idea — but I don't have anything else in the diary, so I'll do it.'

The first one was complete chaos, but doing it changed the chemistry in our brains for a little moment, which was incredible. We felt better instantly!

I've always adored music, and have always turned to it to help me flip the script if I'm having a slightly stressy, anxious day. The right piece of music at the right time can make me feel better (which is quite clever, really).

So, the disco became a really brilliant thing that relieved a lot of stress and tension for all of us — the kids too! It was a real gear shift, like punctuation in our week, and it reminded us which day was Friday at a time when every day felt the same. From then on, Friday was a blast of joyful silliness that cut through the heaviness. And we found a community where everyone was welcome.

I'd do some of my own songs and some covers, and Richard would always make a lovely cocktail for the end. He was the cameraman, filming it all. The kids would be jumping, slumping on the sofa, climbing the walls. It meant they could get up to a bit of mischief, knowing that Mum and Dad were preoccupied. It was communal. It was a precious time.

The disco was making me feel better ... I don't know what our two years of lockdown would have been like if we hadn't had that space to let go a little bit. Doing this has strengthened my relationship with music, reminding me of the fundamentals of why I love doing what I do and why I love music so much. It fixes things.

So, over to you, reader! You kinda know what makes the right disco for you. It's about tunes you love, the music you and your family respond to. It's about what makes you feel better. Once you've got that, just change little things — like the lighting, for starters! Set the mood.

We spend pretty much all our time in the kitchen. We've got a few neon signs, a big disco light, a smoke machine and a disco ball. All these things were already in our kitchen before the pandemic came along. Maybe this shows you what kind of family we are.

Let the kids lead it — that's a good way to start. They'll have lots of songs they love, so let them choose, and let them play the music louder than normal. Don't feel you need to be expert singers or dancers. Even if you're the new Ginger Rogers and Fred Astaire, your kids are not gonna mind what you're doing — they probably won't even be watching. So just go for it! All they will notice is that you're having a nice time — and they'll love the fact that you are.

If I'm ever feeling a bit down, I'll spend half an hour just getting some tunes on. My kids might eye-roll at first, but we'll have fun! Laughing, doing funny dancing and singing songs you love as a family is such a good way to destress. It just never fails. Try it!

YOU WILL NEED:

cardboard

scissors

small cardboard boxes of
   various sizes (screw boxes
   work great for the feet, if
   you have them)

sticky tape

blue and red paint

sandwich bags

sand

corrugated cardboard
   (optional)

sharp pencil

split pins

red and yellow paper

several scoops of love

Kathy, CB Creative Crew

Kathy: The first ever Camp Bestival I remember, we had a huge Mad Hatter's Tea Party. Everyone got roped in; my mum ended up sewing several tablecloths together to make a huge long one to fit the table. We got into loads of mess in my studio, icing giant fake cakes with plaster of Paris and expanding foam, gluing together old teapots, and constructing crazy, towering plates of glittery fake food — much to the disappointment of the hungry children at the show when they saw the spread and discovered that, sadly, all the sandwiches were made of wood and the other treats were inedible.

We have an amazing creative team, headed up by Josie. Our creative crew work incredibly hard to make the shows look brilliant. One of our most-loved festival characters is the Love-Bot. Ever since his first appearance at the show, he has been spreading the love all over Camp Bestival and beyond, and this year he was joined by his sister, the Earth Bot. Each spring, he's awoken from his winter hibernation in our secret storage yard in Dorset, and he trudges down the hill to Lulworth Castle, where he positions himself to welcome all the festival campers. Sometimes he needs a little oil in his joints to get going, but he's always pleased to see us. Once he's in place, we give him a little spruce-up to ensure he's looking his best. He might need a little touch-up of paint, or the odd screw or bolt replacing, and his key winding, and then he's ready to greet you with his best smile.

We are going to make a mini version of him today for you to enjoy at home.

1. First, cut out a flat rectangle of cardboard the full height you want your Love-Bot to be. Arrange your cardboard boxes on it: one for the head, one for the body, and two for the feet. Leave a bit of space above the head for his antenna. If you turn the boxes inside out so that the print is on the inside, then they will be easier to paint.

2. Stick all the boxes on to the rectangular backboard with sticky tape, making sure you can still open the boxes that make up the body and feet.

3. Paint everything blue except for the feet.

4. Open the feet boxes and place a small sandwich bag inside each one. Fill them with sand. Tie up the tops of the bags and tape the boxes closed. These sandbags will weigh the robot down to stop him toppling over. Paint the feet red. If you like, you can paint some corrugated cardboard and use this to cover them for extra texture. Your robot should now stand up.

5. Now for his arms. Each arm will need three rectangles of card. Cut the corners off the rectangles, and then make a hole at either end of each rectangle with a sharp pencil. Choose two rectangles to become his hands, and cut a little spanner shape out of each. If you have a spanner at home, you could use it to draw around; if not, try a 20p coin. If you don't have either, just go freestyle. Attach the arm pieces together with split pins, and then open the body to attach the arms to the torso using more split pins. Once this is done, you can tape his body closed. The arms should be able to move a bit.

6. Use pieces of coloured paper to add the rest of the detail: his eyes, mouth, knobs and dials.

7. Lastly, use some more coloured paper to make a large peace sign for his chest and two small ones for his antennae. Draw around a cup or your roll of sticky tape to make the circles. Stick the large peace sign to his chest, then stick the small ones to the space on the card above his head. Cut away the excess.

8. Now your robot is complete, you just need to
SPREAD THE LOVE.

family feast
CHOCOLATE-DIPPED FLAPJACK

Dave: Samuel Johnson, the man famous for writing one of the first dictionaries in English, described oats as 'food for men in Scotland, horses in England'. The Scots replied, 'England is noted for the excellence of her horses, Scotland for the excellence of her men.'

Don't go feeding these flapjacks to your horses, now, for they will make humans of any nationality very happy indeed. A buttery caramel strewn with oats would be enough for most, but the dark chocolate and sea salt here offset the sweetness. These flapjacks are the perfect companion to a cup of tea (or two). See page 30 for how to make these part of a high tea good enough to woo any stallion (or filly).

1. Preheat the oven to 170°C/gas mark 3¼ and line a 25cm square baking tin with baking parchment. (You can use any shallow baking vessel here; don't go buying one especially just because you can't face the shame of using your 24cm square tin.)

2. Melt the butter in a saucepan over a low heat. This is an important step, as if you just chuck everything in the pan and whack it on the stove, the sugar can burn, and you'll have fallen at the first hurdle.

3. Once the butter is melted, pop the saucepan on your scales and weigh in the sugars, syrup and fine salt. If you're worried the hot pan might melt your scales, then put a small plate on the scales first. It's all worth it, because you just saved yourself washing up a bowl. Just think of the things you can do with all that time!

4. Now weigh the oats into a big bowl (it needs to be big enough to fit the sugary mix and allow for some robust stirring).

5. Return your saucepan to the hob and heat the sugary mix over a medium heat, stirring constantly to homogenise the bejesus out of it. It wants to be smooth and silky, with no visible melted butter. (If you don't know what 'homogenise' means, then look it up; you'll be using it around the house for weeks.) Bring the sugary mix to the boil and continue stirring for a further 2 minutes, then take it off the heat and pour it into the bowl of oats.

6. Stir the flapjack mix until all that syrupy loveliness is hugging the oats in equal measure. Then simply transfer it into the waiting tin and smooth out the top with a utensil of your choice. At this point, I play a game in my head where I pretend I'm a road worker laying a section of motorway. I use a plastic dough scraper to compact and smooth out my oaty road. You don't have to roleplay it, but it does add to the fun.

7. Bake for 18–22 minutes, depending on how chewy you like it. Allow to cool completely for at least 2 hours before cutting into slices.

8. Melt the chocolate in a saucepan over a low heat, then dip the flapjacks into it. Finish with a flamboyant sprinkle of sea salt or sprinkles. These will keep in an airtight container for around a week.

MAKES 12 FLAPJACKS

YOU WILL NEED:

140g butter

85g caster sugar

110g soft light brown sugar

195g golden syrup

a pinch of fine salt

195g rolled oats

195g jumbo oats

300g dark chocolate

flaky sea salt, to finish
  (or whatever sprinkles
  you love)

Dave the Baker

THE MAGIC OF
CAMP BESTIVAL

by Bruce Hay, Camp Bestival

We've been taking the kids to Camp Bestival since they were just a few months old, and it's amazing to see how much their confidence grows and their experiences change every year. From the moment they first walk into the festival fields, you can see their eyes light up as their heads are filled with the sights, sounds, colours and smells around them — it's like they've landed on a new planet.

Even before we had kids, my wife came along with friends and had such an amazing time with the chilled atmosphere, the delicious food on offer, the quietness of the campsites, the lack of queues at the bars, and the fact that you can go to bed early or stay up late without anyone judging you.

When we did have kids, it was a game-changer, and we experienced the festival in a whole new way. You realise that you are surrounded by like-minded parents who are going through the same highs and lows as you, and are more than happy to lend a hand whenever needed — which is especially appreciated as my wife can find herself on her own with the kids while I'm busy working over the weekend.

It's amazing seeing the children grow up with Camp Bestival, and how with each year they find new activities all over the festival site they've never tried before. They really have their imaginations sparked with so many new ideas, skills and experiences, and always come away inspired to make, create and talk about what they're going to be in life, whether it's a circus performer, skateboarder, rock star, artist or nature lover.

Over the years, we've brought lots of friends with their families to the festival, and it's certainly true that the first time you come to Camp Bestival, you realise it's nothing like any other festival experience. You'll find yourselves taking turns to head back to the tent early so the kids can sleep while your partners go out for the night, dressing up with the kids in matching outfits, decorating the trolley where the kids take naps or give their legs a rest, and getting up early to head to your wand-making workshop or go paddleboarding straight after breakfast.

All year round, the children ask about going to the 'camping festival', wanting to be back there, where the rulebooks are ripped up, you can go to bed when you want, eat what you want, and have so much fun it's impossible to pack it all into one day.

We're lucky to be able to go on family holidays in the UK and abroad most years, but Camp Bestival is the one they talk about the most. It really is a highlight of our family year.

TALLULAH MEARS

(12)

I've properly grown up with Camp Bestival, and I'd be absolutely gutted if my parents wouldn't take me. I'd ask Aunty Josie and Uncle Robby to take me instead. I never, ever want to miss it!

One of my first memories was watching Jess Glynn, alternating between my parents' and Uncle Ben's shoulders so as not to miss a second.

We always dress up. One year my brother Christos went as Thor, my sister Jess went as the Red Woman, and I went as the young Gamora — it was so much fun. Marlee (my idol) glued our eyebrows down! Another time, my cousins and I went as the Pink Ladies, and we were interviewed by Sara Cox.

Eli and I always have good fun in our camp; trolley-riding is always good, and we love covering up our friends with grass!

'I always thought taking my kids to a festival would just make me wish I was at one with my friends instead. But going to a festival that's actually designed with families and children in mind is a whole different – and magical – experience. Camp Bestival Shropshire exceeded all expectations for all of us. There truly is something for everyone. Seeing the kids' faces light up minute after minute was a true highlight of the summer.'

'Standing outside the Big Top at 10pm, while my three-year-old went raving with her dad, my eight-year-old demolished a Mr Whippy and I found myself mesmerised by the trapeze act (as the baby slept soundly in a trolley) – this was the moment we all fell in love with Camp Bestival.'

'I can honestly say, I don't think there will ever be a day that I don't call Camp Bestival my second home.'

'It really does feel like coming home.'

'Just wanted to say a massive thank you for giving us a way to induct our daughter into festival life. She, in her own words, "has had her mind blown".'

'Our first ever festival, the furthest we've been away from home, and the best experience my kids and I have had together. There was something for each of us and such a great vibe in general!'

'An amazing, friendly atmosphere, fantastic live music, great entertainment ... My four-year-old grandson decorated all of our faces, the lovely family next to us in the castle arena let my two-year-old grandson share their trolley, and the fireworks and "We Are the Champions" gave me goosebumps. Just everything. My first ever festival at 58 years old; we've already booked it for next year.'

'This is the fab thing about CB: it's totally inclusive to everyone.'

'The very fact that there are things to do for adults and children means we all get to do something we love.'

'We have a 15-year-old boy and an eight-year-old girl. Finding things that we can all enjoy together is getting harder. During The Human League, I had a moment. Our daughter was sitting on her dad's shoulders, our lad was dancing beside me, and all of us were singing our socks off. It made me a little emotional, particularly to see our teen like that. All self-consciousness had gone out the window; he was just belting out the words without a care in the world. It meant so much to me; this must have been such a safe and secure place for him to just let himself go and have fun. It's not easy to do that with your folks when you're 15 and uber cool! So that's why we've been the past two years, and we'll come again next year. Precious togetherness.'

'Spending time together as a family. We arrive at Camp Bestival on Thursday morning and mobile phones, tablets and electronic devices are locked in the car. We have fun and play games and mess around at the tent, then we go and watch an act or visit a tent in the arena. "We Are Family" is our Camp Bestival anthem every year.'

'Our daughter is very easily overwhelmed by lots of activity and noise, and can become distressed. The Dingly Dell is a godsend for us at these times, and we retreated there on several occasions to reset. Usually this can feel very isolating for us, like we have a "difficult" child, but this time we met other parents of children who have similar difficulties, and I think we were all comforted by this.'

'This was my first festival as a single parent. We came alone, but met loads of amazing new friends while we were there. We felt safe and there was definitely no judgement that I was on my own. It's a family-friendly festival that appeals to all types of family, even the non-traditional ones like us.'

'My teenage son took a friend for the first time this year, and it was great to see my son enthusiastically showing him around. They went off to do their own thing and joined up with us later. We've been coming since he was six.'

PETE
BATEMAN,

Caravanserai

After building a few bits and bobs for Bestival, including the archway (which we still use), I came across a very trashed but still beautiful Roma caravan that was waiting to be scrapped. We got the go-ahead to chop it up and used each end as seating at Bestival back on the Isle of Wight.

It worked well, and Josie asked me to create a whole venue out of caravans. Perfect! So, back in France, I put an ad in the local paper asking for old caravans. Soon I had loads. I then found an old derelict waltzer in a field, which we rebuilt as our stage. We collected lots of chairs, tables, lights, signs, bicycles, suitcases, watering cans, cuddly toys and dead plastic flowers, and it all came together to form Caravanserai.

I think I built the kind of place I wanted to hang out in: somewhere tucked away from the rest of the world, with a great eclectic mix of music, circus, art, plenty of comfy seating, and a good bar. It's like a festival within a festival. Once we're open, I rarely leave.

Over the next ten years, there were a fair few changes, and lots of new bits have been added: the Camionettes, the Train of Thoughts, the pods, a new entrance, a bandstand. We've tried different layouts, but always keep the same vibe and ethos. The way it's evolved is often inspired by what I find being thrown away or going cheap. I like the 'surprises' or 'accidents' that can happen when you work like this, and enjoy just responding to whatever turns up. I never quite know how it's going to turn out.

WELCOME TO THE MAGICAL WORLD OF CAMP BESTIVAL!

The brainchild of renowned music specialist Rob da Bank and creative director Josie da Bank, the UK's ultimate family festival is the only one of its kind to cater for parents, tots and teens in equal measure. It's a place where kids get back to nature and families create unforgettable memories together over four adventure-packed days in the great outdoors.

The multi award-winning shows offer hundreds of activities, from bushcraft, circus schools, sports and immersive theatre through to incredible live acts and DJs, family raves and circus spectaculars. Whether you're after wellness, cocktails, award-winning street food or flamboyant cabaret, you can share it all with like-minded families.

Camp Bestival takes place over the summer holidays, at two venues: Lulworth Castle in Dorset and Weston Park in Shropshire.

RESOURCES

WEBSITES

Travel Outlandish (traveloutlandish.com)

Woodland Trust (woodlandtrust.org.uk)

Country File (countryfile.com)

BOOKS

The Almanac: A Seasonal Guide to 2022 by Lia Leendertz

The Twelve Months by Llewelyn Powys

Nature's Calendar: A Month-by-Month Guide to the Best Wildlife Locations in the British Isles, Introduction by Chris Packham

MAGAZINES

BBC Sky at Night

ORGANISATIONS

Shropshire Astronomical Society (shropshire-astro.co.uk)

The UK Space Agency

www.CaMPBestivaL.net

SPRING

MARCH

How to ... Have easier family adventures by Robby da Bank

Make and create: Performance make-up with Isadora

Family feast: High tea with Cirque Bijou, Josie and Dave the Baker

APRIL

How to ... Lessen stress when throwing a party by Fearne Cotton

Make and create: Hedgerow headdress with Spinney Hollow

Family Feast: Big Bestival dinner with Ben and Holly Cooking for 20 on a budget

MAY

How to ... Make it in the music industry (and survive 25 years!) by Mike Cuban (Cuban Brothers)

Make and create: Juggling Balls with Lucas (Bigtopmania)

Family feast: Firepit porridge with Dave the Baker

SUMMER

JUNE

How to ... Make a barbecue more memorable by Chops and DJ BBQ

Make and create: A woodland family with Rhea, Eli, Tao and Zen

Family feast: S'mores with Robby and Miller

JULY

How to ... Dress up and let go! by Ned Able Smith

Make and create: Bum bag with Cheryl Griffiths

Family feast: Mud kitchen fun with Abbie Gadsden

AUGUST

How to ... Have the BEST time at a festival with kids of all ages (and not kill each other!) by Jo Whiley

Make and create: Radish Carving with Ben and Holly

Family feast: Festival breakfast with the Mears Family

AUTUMN

SEPTEMBER

How to ... Live sustainably (through thinking, acting and engaging)

Make and create: Animal Yoga with Laura Lotus

Family feast: Easy One-pot Macaroni Cheese with Lisa Board

OCTOBER

How to ... Make a show to perform with your family by Billy Alwen and Claire Hodgson

Make and create: Skeleton make-up with Robby and Eli da Bank

Family feast: Halloween Feast with the da Bank Family

NOVEMBER

How to ... Create the perfect party playlist by Chris Tofu, Continental Drifts

Make and create: Diwali lanterns with Kathy

Family feast: Cooking on a budget with Ben and Holly

WINTER

DECEMBER

How to ... Decorate your home at Christmas by Josie da Bank

Make and create: Christmas baubles with Cara Kane

Family feast: Turkey on the grill with Chops and DJ BBQ

JANUARY

How to ... Inspire your kids to love music by Kwame Bakoji-Hume

Make and create: Loo-roll rockets with Josie da Bank

Family feast: Three-cheese cauliflower with Fatboy Slim

FEBRUARY

How to ... Have the best kitchen disco by Sophie Ellis-Bextor

Make and create: Love-Bot with Kathy

Family feast: Chocolate-dipped flapjack with Dave the Baker

ACKNOWLEDGEMENTS

Robby and Josie would like to thank (with a great big heart): Anna Bingham, for making sure we deliver and create the book on time, and for all her lovely input; Jo Bennett, for bringing the book to the table; Elizabeth Bond at Penguin, for making the book a reality and for her beautiful enthusiasm for us and Camp Bestival; Lucie Stericker for the art direction, and her patience in waiting for drawings and accepting a big change in direction halfway through; our old mate Jamie Baker, for the fantastic photo shoots over the summer at our home (and the last 20 years); and Victor Frankowski and his team.

Camp Bestival wouldn't be possible without our core team, some of whom have worked with us for 20 years ... Bruce Hay, Cara Kane, Vicki Ludford, Abbie Gadsden, Keith Howison, Becks Clarke, Jenni Jones, Josh Peverley, Kathy Woolley, Pete Callard (the best chippy in town), Phil Ludford, Kate Jackman, Rhea McCarthy, and Jayson and Caroline Perry. A super big thank you to Denis Desmond for keeping the brand alive, and to Simon Moran, Stuart Douglas and Gary Ezard (possibly the most patient man alive), the Live Nation support and backbone. To David Hetherington, Sam Jones, Lucy Camp, Jos and AJ at VIP Nation, and their teams, who go above and beyond every summer, rain or shine. To Alex Hulme for the feasting and food; Alex Brooke and Michael Gwyther for the ace drinks, cocktails and bars; Aimee Ambrose, Andy Grey, Clockwork, and Matt and Steve Widget for sound and lights; James and Sara Weld and all at Lulworth Castle; and Colin, Jenny and Andrea, and all at Weston Park.

The festivals wouldn't be what they are without the incredible artists and creatives who play and create with us every year. We are super blessed to know and have worked with the same folk since we began in 2004: Pete Bateman, the creator of Caravanserai; the High Priest and sonic alchemist Chris Tofu; Billy Alwen and all at Cirque Bijou; Kate and Geoff and the wonderful Spinney Hollow tribe; Richard Cranmer, our firework master and chief pyrotechnic; Laura Gate-Eastley for the yoga; Pete and Lucas Wintercrane; Ben and Holly Cooke; Richard Little; the Raj Circus and brass band; Cosmic Kim; Greg and Hilary Butler with the Pigs' Big Ballroom; the Woodland Tribe; DJ BBQ; Chris 'Chops' Taylor; Dave Fennings; David Wright, the Breaducator; Bobby Lost and all Lost and Found massive and crew; Matt the Hat and the Inflatable Church mayhem masters; the African Activities Crew; and the Textile Junkies, plus many, many more crafters, performers, makers, poets, foodies, talkers and circus folk. Thanks to Sara Cox, Jo Whiley, Norman Cook, Tayo, The Cuban Brothers and Mike Keat, Sophie Ellis-Bextor, Gok Wan, Mr Tumble (Justin has played every Camp B ever!), Mister Maker, Dick and Dom and Goldierocks — just a few of the brilliant artists that regularly have us on our feet dancing ...

And last but not least, we are super lucky to have a loyal and brilliantly supportive bunch of mates and family who come to the shows, year in, year out, helping out along the way. We dedicate this book to our four sons — who are the reason we're even writing a book and running family festivals — Arlo, Merlin, Miller and Elijah, and to our long-suffering parents Sylvia and David, Sue and Chris. Also to cousins Sam and Milly; Ben and Lisa; Lilly and Edward Board; Kate, Ned and Bear; Natasha Dettman and Sean; Sam, Tallulah and David 'Mr' Mears; Ria, Marlee and Mark King; all of Team Gherk; Joe Elkins, Steve and Olive; and Meredith, for continually holding the fort (and home) for over 10 years. Plus many, many more.

Here's to another 20 years ... THANK YOU!

I first met Jamie as a young and cool photographer at a dance music magazine I worked at. I was the new and totally useless, colourblind picture editor ... charged with picking the best photos from the world of raves, festivals and DJ every month from our amazing stable of photographers including Jamie. I was a bit in awe of Jamie's look - chiselled jaw, piercing in his eyebrow and natty dressing. I looked like Worzel Gummidge next to him. The editor Ben who later became my manager decided it would be a good idea that Jamie and I team up. We had fun, sometimes too much fun and me and Jamie became best mates. Jamie's always been there since then ... capturing our wedding on a beach in Scotland, snapping our kids growing up and producing his own beautiful offspring for us to hang out with.

Jamie - we thank you for all your amazing shots, the hours you've put into editing and choosing pics and your endless passion for life.

Robby and Josie x

Kate Winslet

'Camp Bestival is more than just a family weekend it's a place to make colourful, joy filled memories that will last you a lifetime!

'As you turn each page of this inspirational, joyous book, just know ... what you see is EXACTLY what you get at Camp Bestival ... and I wouldn't miss it for the world!'

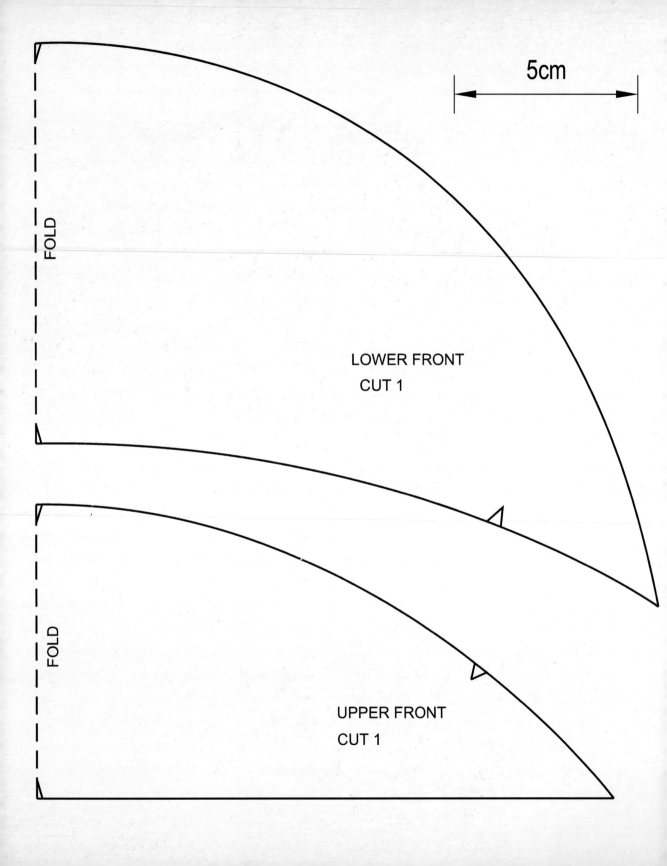

5cm

FOLD

LOWER FRONT
CUT 1

FOLD

UPPER FRONT
CUT 1

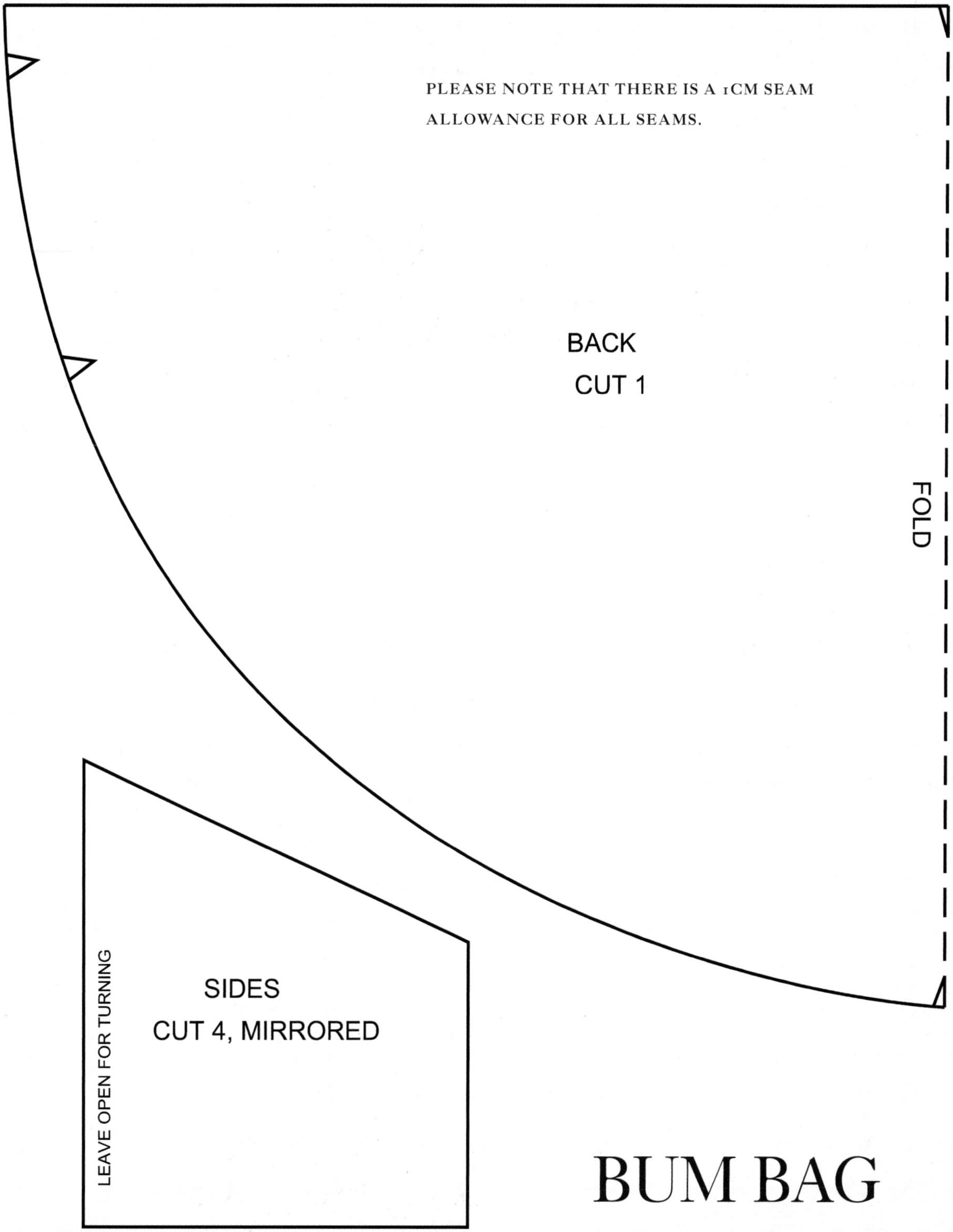

PLEASE NOTE THAT THERE IS A 1CM SEAM
ALLOWANCE FOR ALL SEAMS.

BACK
CUT 1

FOLD

SIDES
CUT 4, MIRRORED

LEAVE OPEN FOR TURNING

BUM BAG

Published in 2024 by Ebury Press, an imprint of Ebury Publishing

20 Vauxhall Bridge Road, London SW1V 2SA

Ebury Press is part of the Penguin Random House group of companies
whose address can be found at global.penguinrandomhouse.com

Design: Studio 7:15

Photography: Jamie Baker/Camp Bestival, Victor Frankowski, Garry
Jones, Leora Bermeister, George Harrison, Livy Dukes, Mike Massaro,
Jordan Curtis Hughes, James Bridle, Gaëlle Beri

Production: Percie Bridgewater

Publishing Director: Elizabeth Bond

Project Editor: Fionn Hargreaves

Copy Editor: Tara O'Sullivan

This edition first published in Great Britain in 2024

www.penguin.co.uk

A CIP catalogue record for this book is available from the British Library

ISBN 9781529925746